ls

Allan Leighton began his car[...] to
become group marketing dir[...]ing
ASDA supermarket chain. There he was credited with [...]nce
described as a basket case into a highly successful company that was sold to
US retail giant Wal-Mart for £6.7 billion in 1999.

When he left his position as president and chief executive of Wal-Mart
Europe he famously coined the phrase 'going plural' as he took on non-
executive positions at a string of companies, including lastminute.com,
BHS, BSkyB and Selfridges. He was the longest serving chairman of
Royal Mail Group until 2009, and is currently non-executive director of a
number of companies. His first book, *On Leadership*, was a bestseller when
it appeared in 2007.

Also by Allan Leighton

On Leadership

Tough Calls

Making the right decisions in challenging times

ALLAN LEIGHTON

BUSINESS
BOOKS

Published by Random House Business Books 2012

2 4 6 8 10 9 7 5 3 1

First published in Great Britain in 2011 by Random House Business Books
Random House, 20 Vauxhall Bridge Road,
London SW1V 2SA

www.randomhouse.co.uk

Addresses for companies within The Random House Group Limited can be found at:
www.randomhouse.co.uk/offices.htm

The Random House Group Limited Reg. No. 954009

A CIP catalogue record for this book
is available from the British Library

ISBN 9781847940544

The Random House Group Limited supports The Forest Stewardship Council (FSC®), the
leading international forest certification organisation. Our books carrying the FSC label are
printed on FSC® certified paper. FSC is the only forest certification scheme endorsed by
the leading environmental organisations, including Greenpeace. Our paper procurement
policy can be found at www.randomhouse.co.uk/environment

MIX
Paper from
responsible sources
FSC® C016897

Typeset in Antique by Palimpsest Book Production Limited,
Falkirk, Stirlingshire
Printed and bound in Great Britain by
CPI Group (UK) Ltd, Croydon CR0 4YY

Contents

Acknowledgements

A big thank you to all of the people who have contributed to this book: your time is much appreciated and this book would not be what it is without your thoughts and perspectives.

Thank you to Teena Lyons who agreed to work with me again following the success of *On Leadership*. Your patience and hard work is greatly appreciated. As always a big thanks to Christine Staveley, my wonderful personal secretary, who once again was in charge of arranging all of the interviews with the contributors – not an easy task.

I would like to thank Gail Rebuck and the team at Random House for their support and, in particular, Nigel Wilcockson who has done a fantastic job on the editing of *Tough Calls*, as well as keeping us all on track and to time (ish!).

Introduction

One of the toughest calls I ever made occurred early on in my career. Having spent 16 years at Mars I didn't think I would ever leave. I hugely admired the family company's values and the way it was run.

Then Archie Norman came knocking at my door and told me about this wonderful opportunity to turn around an ailing super-market group called Asda. As I recall, what he actually said was that things weren't as bad as they seemed to those on the outside, despite all indications to the contrary.

After weeks of due diligence and talks late into the night with Archie, I came close to making what I always knew would be a life-changing decision. Weighing on my mind though was a scenario that had played out only five years earlier, when I had nearly succumbed to a very persuasive offer from Grand Metropolitan. The food, drink and leisure giant had wooed me over a period of months and had offered an incredibly generous package to overcome many of my reservations about taking the leap to join them. Indeed, they had bent over backwards to help me make my decision and even agreed to alter the company's relocation policy to accommodate the needs of my then young family. After secretly attending Grand Met's sales conference in the south of France my mind was made up. I wanted to join this inspirational forward-thinking company and all I had to do was tell my boss.

After an anxious weekend, I drove to work at dawn on the Monday morning. Steeling myself, I strode as confidently as I could into my bosses' office to break the news. They sat in silence as I explained how much I had enjoyed working at Mars, what a fabulous opportunity it had been and how greatly I admired the company. I went on to outline the scope of my job with Grand Met, why it was so exciting and why I thought that I should take it in order to develop my own career.

I eventually ran out of steam and stopped talking. The ensuing silence was deafening. In fact all I could hear was the rhythmic ticking of a clock, the factory rumbling in the distance and the sound of my own blood pounding in my ears.

Eventually, after what seemed like hours but was in fact only a minute or so, my bosses looked at each other. They didn't exchange words, but I could see they had somehow come to an accord. As I shuffled my feet awkwardly in expectation, they stood up.

'We have decided that we will not let you go. We will give you some time to think this through properly.' Every syllable of the word 'properly' was emphasised.

Then they both walked out, closing the door behind them with an ominous clang and locking it. Looking through the frosted glass of the door panel, I saw them give one last glance back into the room as they pocketed the key. I watched the slightly distorted shapes of the pair as they strode purposefully away down the corridor.

I was utterly dumbfounded. I had expected many different reactions; indeed I had mentally rehearsed answers to quite a number of them over the past few days. But this?

I was left locked in that room for four hours, which, as I discovered, was plenty of time to reconsider my options. As the minutes ticked by, I weighed up what I had done so far at Mars, what I still could do there and what I might do at Grand Met.

Eventually I decided to stay. I have since often asked myself why I made that decision. I think it was because there was a nagging doubt inside me. Yes, this was a great opportunity, but I hadn't yet achieved all at Mars that I had set out to do. The timing wasn't right. If I had to put a figure on it, I suspect that I was only 40 per cent convinced about the move to Grand Met. That clearly wasn't enough to swing things.

The percentages were very different when I made my mind up to join Asda. Archie and I had had so many conversations about what we would do with the business if we were both in it together and I could already imagine what we could achieve. We were on the same wavelength, with the same vision.

On paper my two career decisions seem bizarre. I turned down a great opportunity with a great company but accepted an uncertain future with one that was on the ropes. Why? If you asked me now I would say that while with Grand Metropolitan I was only 40 per cent certain that the move was the right one, with Asda the percentage was more like 51 per cent. And my rule of thumb is that if you are at least 51 per cent convinced, based on what you know and what you feel, then that's probably good enough, even if 49 per cent of you is screaming, *Don't do it!* If the percentage of doubt is any higher, then it probably is the wrong decision.

But, of course, that only gets you so far. Within that mix of 'what you know and what you feel' there are all sorts of variables, and, as we are all only too aware, it's not uncommon to make entirely the wrong decision on the basis of what seemed right at the time. After all, every one of us makes decisions every day and while most of them are pretty straightforward and simple, every so often there are some really tough calls that we may get wrong. In business, the daily choices that executives have to make can sometimes be even tougher, the 'right' one leading to acclaimed success, the 'wrong' one resulting in failure that might even end in the break-up or sale of a company and the loss of many jobs and livelihoods. What's more, if you are a leader it's almost invariably the difficult decisions that end up on your desk. If everything is ticking along nicely, most people don't need to bother their boss. It's only when the waters get choppy that people turn to you for help. This generally happens at 3 pm on a Friday, just when everyone is 'tuning down' for the weekend; you think you've survived another week and then the phone rings or somebody looking ashen-faced turns up at your desk. Inevitably, therefore, more than 90 per cent of your time is taken up working on things that are not going well. The decisions you make *are* going to be difficult ones, and you have to be fully aware of their potential consequences.

In *Tough Calls*, I wanted to explore how some of our best-known business leaders make these crucial decisions. I know, from experience, that captains of industry have very different ways of leading, but I have always been curious to see whether there is a common thread linking the thought processes of those at the top, and whether in 'tough times' that changes.

To do this, I asked some of our brightest and best business minds to focus on specific tough calls they have made in the past and describe how they made them, taking me through the deliberating process and assessing the facts that were known at the time, any uncertainties that there might have been and the advice they received from others. I then asked them whether, with the benefit of hindsight, they thought they had made the right decision or whether, given their time again, they would have done things differently.

For these sorts of people, decision making is second nature, and that means that the word 'intuition' or 'gut' often cropped up in the course of our conversations: a decision was made because it was 'felt' to be the right thing to do. That doesn't mean, though, that leaders were making choices on a whim. 'Intuition' turned out to be a finely honed skill that involved a number of thought processes often working at such speed that even the person having them didn't necessarily or consciously break them down into their component parts every time. I'm certainly aware in my own case that what I describe as my gut instinct has actually been years in the making and is in part a product of past experiences – what has worked, what hasn't, and what might not have worked last time but could do so this time.

I should emphasise, though, that there is a big difference between 'experience' and 'experiences', which is why I believe age and experience in themselves are not necessarily the most crucial elements of good decision-making. I know people in their forties and fifties who are experienced, but who haven't had many 'shaping' experiences. I know people in their twenties and thirties whose 'experiences' make them highly qualified to make tough calls. It's what you have encountered along the way, rather than how much time you have spent on the way, that counts.

This complicated mix of thoughts and emotions is very powerful. On occasion it can lead you astray, perhaps encouraging you to make a decision too quickly or without considering other options. On the other hand, I have to say that if you are too easily persuaded by others to ignore your gut instincts completely, you can find yourself signing up to a course of action in which you don't fully believe and then bitterly regretting it when things don't turn out quite the way you had hoped. Every time I've gone against my gut feelings I've regretted it. And, of course, sometimes the decision really can only be made by you. That was certainly true for me when I made my career moves, and I'm intrigued how often leading businessmen cite a decision to take or turn down a particular job as one of the toughest calls they've had to make. Here, for example, is Sir Terry Leahy thinking back to 1997 when he was offered the top job at Tesco:

> One of the toughest decisions I had to make in my whole career was whether to take the Tesco CEO job or not. I gave really serious thought to turning it down and very nearly did. I was not sure whether I could do the job.
>
> The positive side to these early doubts is that it forced me to think through whether I really understood what the job would entail. I had to think what I was going to do when I got the job and whether my ambitions focused on the future of the company, not just on my own advancement. I also knew that if I failed, I would fail spectacularly and publicly; plus I would spend most of my time dealing with problems, because in a

large company there are an enormous number of external stakeholders, such as the government, regulators, NGOs, the press and so on. The other issue was that I knew that I would have to sacrifice a lot of time with my family. Truthfully, even after I talked it through with my wife, I still had a heavy heart when I accepted the job.

I always think that people who take senior jobs without thinking twice often wake up and think, 'What am I going to do now?'

When a successful leader talks about relying on their intuition or their gut instinct, I suspect that they are mentally sifting a range of options or previous experiences, selecting one that might work well, testing it, refining it and then going for broke. This may all be such second nature to them that they're not consciously aware of the processes they're going through, but I suspect that many good decision-makers would concur with General Lord Richard Dannatt, one of the two former heads of the British Army I talked to in the course of writing *Tough Calls*, when he brilliantly summarises successful decision-making in the following terms:

In my line of work, we separate out what has to be done into three levels: the strategic, the operational and the tactical. Most firms seem to have the strategic bit ticked off and have strategies for just about everything. Probably too many strategies in my book.

The tactical level is all about delivery, or making it happen. However, there is an important bit in between the ideas and the action. It is the operational, or campaign, level, which turns ideas into action. That is the bit where the key decisions are taken. Deciding on the plan is the level where you really prove your mettle and which separates the exceptional leaders from the mediocre. It requires serious intellectual rigour.

If there is time, it is always good to war game your plan on a 'what if' basis. You ask, 'Well, we think this is going to happen, but what if the enemy does this? Should we then do this? What if this? What if that?' It is a time-consuming thing to do but I would always do it at the start of a major undertaking, and if I was launching a major business initiative I would do the same.

You make a plan and you think how things are going to go, but there is always a whole bunch of things that might go differently to what you expect. Experience should tell you what might go differently but then you try to think, 'Well if that does go differently, how would we change?' If you have done your 'what iffing' properly, then a fair number of your contingencies will come up, but you and your team will be ready for them.

The approach of this book follows Lord Dannatt's decision arc. The first few chapters look at the nature of the decision that needs to be made (the strategic); then there are ones on how people road-test the decision they have made (the 'what if' stage); finally attention is turned to the way in which decisions are executed (the operational and tactical). In reality going through all these stages may occupy a few seconds or a number of hours or several weeks, but great decision-makers touch all the bases somewhere along the way.

The word 'decision', of course, covers a multitude of possibilities – I can make a decision to wear a particular shirt, to attend a particular meeting, or to buy or sell a particular company. These decisions are very different from one another in terms of scale and importance. But they're also very different from one another in terms of the thought-processes and strategies they involve. There is no one-size-fits-all approach here. In most cases, for example, you have to act positively and decisively. A decision *not* to go with a takeover opportunity, on the other hand, could prove a very shrewd move. In many cases, you need to be in full possession of the facts before you act. In some instances, though, time won't be on your side: you have to act very quickly even though not all the facts are known. In a large number of cases you can survive the wrong decision, but there are always some from which there is no return.

Given all these variables, I've decided to group different types of decision into categories. The first is the radical decision – when things within an organisation's control have gone badly wrong and urgently need addressing or when a major shift in strategy is required to keep a company on course. The second is the crisis decision – when external factors take over and you are hit by a challenge or a disaster that was not of your making but that becomes your problem. Then comes the opportunity decision – you have the chance to take advantage of something that crops up (perhaps a potential takeover or merger) and you have to decide whether to go for it or not. And finally there is the progress deci sion – the sort of smaller-scale decision businesses face every single day; it might not involve radical change but the wrong deci sion could prove deeply damaging over time. These categories each share particular characteristics, just as they differ in certain details from the others.

One thing they do all have in common, though, is that they are impossible to call correctly every single time. No leader I have ever spoken to has claimed that they get things right 100 per cent of the time. All make mistakes. All have to back-pedal or change direction occasionally. My own view is that it does not matter if you are not 100 per cent right, 100 per cent of the time. In fact you won't be. Even being right 70 per cent of the time is a pretty good average. Arguably, this is just as well. If there really was a perfect solution to every problem every time, it could actually prove debilitating: we'd be spending so much time trying to work out what that perfect solution was that we'd never do anything.

Good decision-makers know that they will sometimes make mistakes. Their success arises from keeping these mistakes to a minimum, acknowledging them swiftly and then learning from them. They also know that providing a sense of impetus and progress is often more critical than agonising for months about the nuances of a particular decision. Moreover they know that there may be more than one way to achieve a desired goal. That means that if things do go wrong – and they will – they don't give up. They try a different approach.

You could say that this was a lesson I learned at a very young age. As a teenager I was a huge fan of The Doors, and when I heard they were playing a gig in London I decided that whatever happened I had to be there. I went to ask my parents for some money for the train fare and just got a lecture about being only 15 years old and too young to go off to see wild rock bands. Undeterred, I asked my uncle and he kindly lent me £2. It more than covered the price of the tickets, which were only 50p each, but, sadly, it was not enough for my bus or train fare.

I sat down to work out what I could do to make my dream happen and decided that the only way to get there was to get on my bike. Literally. I worked out it would take two days to get there from my home in Oxford and so set off at nightfall, 48 hours before the concert. I had no lights for my bicycle, and had to strap a torch on my handlebars. All in all, though, I thought things were going pretty well. That was, until I was picked up by the police four hours into my journey and taken straight back to where I had come from.

After enduring the inevitable lecture from my parents, who were not too impressed to be woken up in the middle of the night by the police, I made my position clear. As soon as they went back to bed, I was going to try again. There was nothing they could do to stop me. By this stage, they were so exhausted, or perhaps they were moved by my determination, that they gave in and gave me my bus fare.

Good decision-makers understand that if the goal is clear, there may be more than one way to achieve it. They also understand timing. Not all decisions have to be made at breakneck speed. Sometimes it is prudent to sit on your hands for a while because you know that you need just a bit more data and that time is on your side. You might not have the luxury of four or five days, but you might be able to afford four or five hours, and that could be just long enough for you to penetrate the thick fog of battle and filter out the distracting noise and disorienting sense of urgency. Pausing for breath before you make a judgement is rarely the wrong thing to do. Sometimes, in fact, having given yourself that breathing space, you might even find that you don't need to make a decision at all and that things are sorting themselves out without requiring your intervention. Former Prime Minister Harold Macmillan famously had a notice put up outside his office that read 'Calm deliberation untangles every knot'. It's certainly true that rushed decision-making achieves nothing.

The other thing I have learned is that good decision-makers are decisive. It sounds obvious, but it isn't. Once they've decided what they want to do, however borderline their deliberations may have been, they stick with it. They don't look back. They make sure that everyone commits to what has been agreed. If, further down the line, they need to make adjustments or change course, then they're canny enough to do so. But unless there is a positive reason to change, they don't.

Writing *Tough Calls* has given me an opportunity to look back at my own career and also to reflect on how much the world has changed since I wrote my first book *On Leadership* in 2007. Back then, save for a handful of lone voices predicting that the boom years were nearly over, the corporate world was riding high. It is hard to comprehend how much has changed in those four short years and how most of us have coped or not in getting through this extraordinary economic time. I defy anyone to say it hasn't been a huge jolt to the system. It swept each and every one of us off our feet.

We've all coped with various corporate crises in the past. We've been through slowdowns, housing crises, seen the Internet bubble burst and the usual short-term blips. But this one has proved far bigger. Everybody's bubble burst at the same time and that had never happened to any of us before. It won't go away overnight either. It will have an impact on us for years to come. It will take a very long time to clear up this financial tsunami, and just as coastlines are transformed by tsunamis, so the corporate world will never look the same again. Most people I know are saying it's the toughest climate they have ever had to work in, with lots of unchartered waters.

Can we learn anything from it? I'd like to think so. In truth, the world collectively made a series of appalling large-scale decisions. Let's hope that if we all pay more attention to the way in which we make tough calls in the future, this won't happen again. That's what this book is about.

Part 1:
Making a Tough Call

Chapter One
The Radical Decision

It was 2002. I had joined the Royal Mail in March and spent a fair amount of time out on the road with the posties who did all the work. I was now back at the London head office, ready to talk to the people who *thought* they did most of the work. There was a lot to put right. The Royal Mail was losing £1 million a day. The organisation was plagued by strikes and virtually crippled by years of bad management and under-investment. Meanwhile, competitors were picking off all the best bits of the business by introducing their own, more efficient, systems. We needed to make some key strategic decisions.

I began by asking if there were any existing strategy papers and, if so, if I could see them. Within a few days dozens of cardboard boxes filled to the brim with documents had poured into my office, so many in fact that it became increasingly difficult to move around. Ultimately, some 1,000 grand-looking papers containing the word 'strategy' and covering every conceivable angle littered my floor. I was gobsmacked. The Royal Mail had more strategies than any company I had ever seen in my whole life. Indeed if you had put all the strategies of all the companies I had ever had contact with into a big pile, they would still have been dwarfed by the Royal Mail collection. For a short while I started to believe that we might even have more strategies than we had letters to deliver.

I also discovered that the pride and joy of the organisation was its balanced scorecard. Now, for those of you not familiar with this management tool, a balanced scorecard is a strategic planning and management system that sets out the vision and strategy of a company and monitors its performance against specific goals. Often the data is depicted as a traffic light system which indicates how close the company is to meeting these strategic goals by awarding it a red, amber or green light according to how well it is doing. In the Royal Mail's case, strategy seemed to have become a strategic goal all on its own.

Bracing myself to dig a little deeper, I asked for a copy of the Royal Mail's organisational chart. In particular I wanted to know how many people had the term 'strategy' in their job title. Sure enough, the chart duly arrived and it emerged that there were 700 people boasting that they were a strategic executive for this or that. The reason for this plethora of supposed strategic experts was that if a person had 'strategy' or 'strategic' in their job title, then they got more Hay Points. The more Hay Points they had, the higher their pay package. Therefore there was a strategy and a person in charge of that strategy for every part of the business.

The fact that seemed to escape the team that eagerly showed me the key indicators of their strategic reports was that every single traffic light was stuck on red. Clearly, out of the hundreds of strategies littered around the place, none had even come close to working.

How could this have happened? How could strategy have become an industry all of its own? It emerged that part of the problem was down to the way the business had been managed by previous governments. Or not managed. Ministers had, in the past, asked for a strategy for this or that and Royal Mail executives had been able to breathlessly wave a paper for it and say it was in hand.

The end result was an organisation with a 95 per cent market share and with strategies coming out of its ears. Unfortunately, it was also an organisation that was haemorrhaging money and that was on the verge of collapse. On paper, all those strategies sounded great. In reality, they meant nothing.

Not unnaturally, I went ballistic. Here was a basket case of a company that had more strategies than any other on the planet but no plan for pulling itself out of the mess that it was in. And yet both the problem and the solution were breathtakingly straight-forward. If you're losing £1 million a day, you need to stop losing £1 million a day. You do that by saving money. In the case of the Royal Mail, that meant fewer people, no strike days, practically no capital expenditure and the end of the very expensive second daily postal delivery service. You also find ways of making money – in this case by growing the European parcels business. That was it.

In my first 12 months in the job I junked the ludicrous Consignia name introduced 16 months earlier, one of the most ridiculous and ill-judged corporate makeovers ever known. We reverted to calling the organisation Royal Mail, a name everyone was proud of. I restructured the company, streamlining it from 15 different busi-nesses to five, stripped away layers of management, took steps to stamp out bullying, brought in former FA boss Adam Crozier as chief executive, and announced 30,000 redundancies.

Anyone reading this will think, well that is obvious, isn't it? You don't need to be a genius to come up with this set of decisions or a cost-cutting strategy. They'd be right, of course, but the fact is that up until the moment someone set out what Royal Mail needed to do to survive, no one there had ever even considered what was proposed as a possibility. Over time a culture had grown up that had lost sight of what the business was for and where it was heading. People were making decisions, certainly, but they were worse than wrong decisions; they were irrelevant ones. Few were aware just how close to the edge the Royal Mail was tottering, and the few who did didn't see what this had to do with them.

And there in a nutshell you have the two classic elements of tough calls in a company in crisis. It's clear what the problem is, it's clear in broad outline what needs to be done, but the chances are that those on the inside are too much in denial or too obsessed with irrelevant strategy to look at the bigger picture. Companies don't die; people kill them. Complacency and arrogance are usually the weapons of death.

You can see this scenario playing out over and over again. Take the financial crash of 2008, for example. All the evidence was there. You could see that house prices were rising unsustainably around the world, especially in places like the UK, Ireland and the US, fuelled by high-risk, high-debt equity mortgages. You could see that certain economies were running huge balance of payments deficits and relying too much on consumer expenditure. You could see that there were big concentrations of risk on the balance sheets of many banks. Those who were in a position to do something about this, however, couldn't see it coming. They were not wilfully blind. They were arrogant, complacent and simply too embedded in the problem to see it.

This very common situation helps to explain why companies in crisis so often need an outsider to put them right. The outsider may be no wiser, but he or she is sufficiently objective to be able to identify the problems relatively easily and carries no baggage.

A classic example of this is the way in which Lou Gerstner pulled IBM back from the brink in the early 1990s. IBM had pretty much led the computing world since 1964, but then it all went horribly wrong. Revelling in its reputation for being perfectly managed and in tune with its customer, it became complacent and so missed out on the rise of the personal computer. By the time Gerstner was parachuted in, the company was losing billions. Gerstner had an outsider's cool judgement. He could see what was wrong and why it had gone wrong, and he could see a way forward, too. The company needed to go back to basics. He capitalised on IBM's greatest strength – the integration of hardware, software and services – slashed the headcount and took on the internal factions that were dragging the company down. In his eight years at the helm the company grew by 40 per cent. It wasn't rocket science, but it worked.

Fewer big, not more small decisions

When you're dealing with a major problem, the first challenge is to boil it down to a few executable solutions. Make too many decisions and chaos will ensue. Focus on the key issues and you're far more likely to achieve success.

My early time at Asda is a classic example. I very nearly didn't take up the offer of a job there because the scale of the task ahead was so daunting. I started my career at Mars and had spent 18 highly enjoyable years there. Mars was a solid, well-run, highly profitable, established company with some of the best brands in the world. It was also teeming with rank upon rank of some of the most talented brains in the fast-moving consumer goods (FMCG) business arena. Indeed, such was the power of the Mars training and development programmes, that Past Marsters, as those from the Mars stable have been dubbed, developed a reputation, which endures to this day, for keeping things simple, focusing on the important stuff, getting things done, and remembering that people are a company's biggest asset. Asda, sadly, was the precise opposite.

In 1992, when Archie Norman first began talking to me about joining Asda, the supermarket chain was imploding. It was weighed down by a number of ill-thought-out acquisitions through the 1970s and 80s, many of which were not even related to the food business, and was further impeded by an unnecessarily hierarchical and bureaucratic structure which seemed designed to keep the management as far away as possible from the people who actually did the work. It was struggling to pay its bills on time or, indeed, at all. Few people at the top of the business seemed to know what was going on, or what to do about it. No wonder people in the stores called the company headquarters in Leeds the 'dream factory'.

The many problems, then, were very apparent. What was needed, though, was not a basket of solutions but a handful of clearly targeted ones. Fortunately, my time at Mars, which counted Asda as one of its biggest customers, had given me a ringside seat to view what was really going on. As a highly organised, customer-focused business, Mars had reams of research on all its customers and products and the section on Asda did not make pleasant reading. Time and again, our research showed that the supermarket chain had completely lost its way with its customers. Here was a chain that had built a reputation on 'Asda price', basing its success on a strategy of selling high volumes at a low margin which were great value for money. Everyone remembered with fond nostalgia the evocative shot of a contented shopper happily patting the change in her back pocket. Yet by the time we joined Asda it was offering anything but good value.

Such was the scale of the problem that it was tempting to run around like a headless chicken trying to come up with a wealth of strategies to fix anything and everything all at once, and fast. What we did, though, was take a deep breath and remind ourselves that we needed to focus on a major issue that would really make a difference. In Asda's case it was clearly getting 'Asda price' back on track. All that required was the relatively simple device of lowering our prices so that we once again became the best-value grocer on the block.

Most businesses that have been or are successful on a continuing basis have what I call a 'Business System.' In Asda's case it was larger stores than anyone else, which could drive more volume per store than anyone else, which required lower prices than anyone else. Without any of these three in place 'system failure' occurs and, generally, the business model – and the business itself – implodes. Asda's move from guaranteeing lower prices than anyone else literally meant that one of the wheels had fallen off and the bus had headed for the kerb.

All great failures were once a great success. Getting back to the 'system of success' or 'back to the future – with modernity' is often all that's required to restore success over time. The simplest tough call is: Let's go back to what we used to be.

Adam Crozier, who, like me, began his career at Mars, says that it was his second job, at advertising giant Saatchi & Saatchi, where he learned one of his most valuable lessons in this respect. He had become joint chief executive of Saatchis at a time of crisis, after the eponymous founders Charles and Maurice Saatchi had been pushed out by American shareholders. Adam had to find a way to steady the ship in a very short space of time and took his cue from the job that people in his organisation were doing every day.

> In advertising people give you an enormous amount of information about a product, or a company, or its market and that has to be edited down to what is important so it can be got across to the target audience in 30 seconds. Funnily enough I've found that this is a really applicable skill for lots of other things. What we are all doing is taking a series of very complicated issues and hundreds of different priorities and honing them down to concentrate on just two or three things that will really make a difference.

How do you get that clarity? In my view, you don't get it by holing yourself up in your office, reading dozens of reports and studying the statistics. That comes later. What you need to do first is get out there and talk with people – both frontline staff and customers. Note the words 'talk with', not 'to' or 'at'. Most people get talked at and so tend not to respond. If you talk 'with' them it means that you're in listening rather than talking mode, and that you're on their wavelength. People respond to those who they know are really listening to them: they think that if they're listened to, something might actually happen! And they have something useful to say. They have a way of latching on to the essentials:

'We're doing this and no one seems to like it'; 'Why don't you do that any more?' They may not give you the single answer you're looking for – in fact, they'll probably give you a hundred – but they'll almost certainly provide you with that light-bulb moment when you say to yourself, 'I can see why it's gone wrong, and I can see what I need to do to put it right.'

Keeping the focus

Inevitably, focusing on one or two key decisions means parking other ones, and a major challenge that many leaders encounter is not to be distracted by other decisions that they could make and that others might be urging on them. Stephen Hester at RBS offered me a classic instance of this. In November 2008, he came under the most extraordinary public scrutiny when he was para-chuted in to turn around the RBS banking group. His appointment was made at the height of the credit crunch and emotions were understandably running high. That year the bank had hardly been off the front pages, having undergone the largest rights issue in British corporate history and taken a £37 billion injection of cash from the UK treasury to avert the complete collapse of the finan-cial sector. To add to the pressure, everyone appeared to have firm views about what needed to be done.

Early on, Stephen was approached with many suggestions for turning the bank around, including numerous entreaties to consider rebranding some of the bank's facia. Many years of take-overs and consolidation in the banking world had left the group with a range of different subsidiaries, including National Westminster

Bank, Coutts, Ulster Bank and Direct Line. Internationally there were quite a number of brand names, too. The thinking from many people was that, as the bank was undergoing a fresh start, it was an ideal time to consolidate the portfolio and create a strong central brand.

At one level, you can understand why people should have urged Stephen to do something about this. Indeed, if the bank had been doing well it would have been a logical thing to consider: companies rightly agonise about the best way to handle their branding. But, as Stephen rightly points out, to have made decisions about branding when the issue of basic survival was on the table would have been a distraction:

> At that stage, the ability for RBS to survive at all financially was in question. The ability for it to serve its customers consistently was, as a consequence, in question. The prospects the shareholders, including the government, had of getting money back was in question. So the overwhelming priority had to be to attend to those key business issues. People came to me to talk about branding for RBS, saying there was a need for some tag line, or branding or new advertising campaign. I said, 'No'. Branding is important and the way you present yourself externally is important, but, on our list of priorities, spending a lot of time on that was not even close. There was no immediate business benefit.

Adam Crozier had a very similar experience at Royal Mail:

> I remember in the first year at the Royal Mail, when we were looking at the budgets, I found that we had 2,427 different projects going on. Just imagine how much time, energy and loss

of focus was going into trying to make all of that happen. Everyone had their own pet projects and pet budgets. One of the toughest jobs I had was stopping all of that. That sounds as though it should have been easy, but actually it was incredibly difficult. In the end I had to say, 'Just stop. That won't help. I get that these projects are all terribly interesting, but they won't get us anywhere.'

We had to get to a point where there were a handful of key things that we devoted our energies into trying to do.

I've looked here at two companies in crisis, but it's worth remembering that the same rule applies even to very successful businesses. Make too many decisions and the results can be confusing and even self-contradictory. They create white noise that can distract from the real issues and, in time, damage the company. It's much more important to execute a well-conceived strategy than try to prove how innovative you are by constantly embarking on new ones. Take Marks & Spencer, for example. While Sir Stuart Rose was at the helm he was the recipient of constant new ideas and proposed new strategies. In fact, he calls M&S a 'taxi driver' business, because anybody and everybody has an opinion. Unfortunately, while this might be viewed as flattering by some, it is unnecessarily distracting.

Everybody thinks they have an opinion on how to run M&S. The news is everyone's opinion is different. One likes the chicken jalfrezi, someone else likes this and someone else hates that. Everyone quite likes the brand, but none of them will agree on which bit they like. It is like listening to the chatter of an opinionated cab driver from the back of a taxi.

Some companies by definition generate a disproportionate amount of noise and you have got to accept that that is the case. It does affect you, but you have to do what you believe to be right.

Someone has to say, 'Well I have listened to what you all have to say and you are not all going to be totally happy. However, this is my view of what roughly you all want and this is what I am going to do.'

DECISION-MAKING LESSONS

› Not making a decision is the worst decision you can make. You must always make a decision even if you are not 100 per cent sure. Procrastination is damaging.
› Don't react to every single issue and nuance in the belief you have to make a choice. If you get distracted by all the noise that goes on in an organisation you will never get anything done.
› If you only ever make one mistake you are not pushing the boundary. The trick is not to make the same mistake twice.

Sir Stuart Rose, former chairman and chief executive, Marks & Spencer

Sticking to your guns

Making a decision – particularly a major one – requires both focus and resolve. Sticking with it in the teeth of opposition and criticism similarly requires considerable courage. As Stuart Rose's comment on M&S shows, most people have an opinion about most things. Even the most minor of decisions will find a critic somewhere. And when you're faced with a major strategic shift the number of critics multiplies exponentially. As I know all too well, when a large organisation like Asda or Royal Mail has been staggering along for years, the media will gleefully document every single one of its convulsions. Moreover, in the modern world of social media, blogging, texting, tweeting and goodness knows what, you can rest assured that someone, somewhere will be only too happy to constantly fan the flames with an endless supply of disinformation and intrigue.

What makes this particularly difficult in companies that are struggling is that the chances are that much of the opposition will come from within. While the problems – and the solutions – may seem obvious to you and to many who stand outside the company, it's unlikely that everything will seem so crystal clear internally. There will be a large number of people who have worked at the company for a long time who wholeheartedly believe they have worked hard and have done a good job and who will regard any break with the past as a rejection of their careers and achievements. If no one told them that they were doing things wrong before, why should they change now? Moveover, they say to themselves, why should we trust the new decision-makers any more than we did the last lot?

This can be very disconcerting. After all, many of the people questioning your decision are able and keen. They may have super-ficially very plausible reasons why they think what you are doing is wrong. What's more, many of them will be in positions where they have constant access to you and so can confront you with their forceful views – often with other influential people present. You really have to be able to keep your nerve when you're faced with such remorseless negativity.

According to Justin King, chief executive at Sainsbury's, the existing team at a struggling company will tend to fall into three camps.

> There will be those who quickly become genuine, signed-up card-carriers to the new direction. There will be those who will give it a go, but actually feel a bit uncomfortable with it and need to be helped, encouraged, trained and developed until they accept the change. And then there are internal terrorists. These are the people who are just resolutely waiting for the next lot to come in with yet another plan and sit it out by sniping from the sidelines.
>
> Internal terrorists are the worst kind of people to have around. They'll tell you that you have made the greatest deci-sion in the world, whilst privately thinking everything is a terrible decision and telling everyone around them the same. Their words tell you everything is great, whereas their actions show you it is the other way around. That is extremely damaging. They have to go.

It may sound harsh, but these internal terrorists do need to be sought out and got rid of at the earliest opportunity. This sort of decisive action provides a much-needed visible trauma. It gives a

DECISION-MAKING LESSONS

› When people ask me what makes a
  good chief executive, I say relentlessness.
  The job is relentless. It comes at
  you relentlessly and you have to be
  relentless in your decision-
  making. You have to be prepared for
  that.
› Keep listening, all the time, even
  after a decision has been made. But
  never let it get in the way of being
  resolute.
› Always remain firmly attached to a
  decision right up until the point that
  you say it is the worst decision that you
  have ever made.

Justin King, Sainsbury's

sense of electricity, a 5,000-volt shock, which says this is for real, not just another piece of management rhetoric. There is no point everyone keeping their heads down and thinking this too will pass, because it clearly won't. The old organisation is fractured. Things and people need to change.

Moving people around and getting rid of the bad apples sends a clear message: the people who remain are not going to be treated the same way as in the past, they may well not be reporting to the same person, and they certainly won't be fed the same message. Put simply, from now on they have got to work differently. Unless a new leader is that radical and forceful, he or she doesn't stand a chance: all the things that caused the problem in the first place will gradually leach back into the organisation and paralyse it. In some cases, as Justin argues, you actually have to shift the whole culture of the organisation in order to shake things up on a more everyday level:

> Culture is like an elastic band. It is, of course, possible to move culture, but actually there is this incredible dynamic in most large organisations that grips on to one end of the band hard. It desperately wants to pull it back to where it once was, because any sort of change is difficult and painful.
>
> What happens is that the further you stretch the culture, the more – not less – the organisation wants to pull the band back where it once was.
>
> For true cultural change, you have to stretch the elastic band so far that it breaks completely and there is no longer any point people holding on to it like grim death.

If the band snaps, then there will inevitably be casualties and some, possibly many, will have to go. This may sound very harsh. The fact of the matter, though, is that in a turnaround, radical surgery is often required. There is an imperative for change. A company in trouble can't afford to wait five years while it sends everyone on training programmes or tries to persuade them of the need to change. It has to get on with it. The radical way generally means bringing in a lot of new people. In my first five years at Asda, two-thirds of the management team changed because the company was so fractured we really needed a complete break with the past.

When it comes to more successful companies having to make a radical decision, the chances are that the voices of opposition will be outside the organisation, rather than inside, but that doesn't mean that they are any less distracting. And that can make the instigators of even the best thought-through of decisions think twice.

I found this out for myself some years ago as a non-executive director of Dyson. In 2002, Dyson was riding high as a classic British manufacturing success story. The inventor James Dyson, as he was then (he was knighted in 2006), epitomised the much-loved story of the plucky British underdog who takes on the establishment and wins. It seemed everyone knew the story of how he had relentlessly worked through 5,127 prototypes before finally perfecting his innovative dual cyclone bagless vacuum cleaner which then transformed the market. Having conquered Japan, fought off rivals attempting to copy the idea and overcome numerous legal obstacles, the brand was taking the UK by storm.

Dyson's manufacturing plant in Malmesbury, Wiltshire was a shining beacon for all those who bemoaned that, as a country, Britain just doesn't make anything any more. Here was a factory employing hundreds of people and actually making something customers wanted. Lots and lots of things, in fact, that were being exported all over the world. Commentators were further buoyed up by the fact that James Dyson was such a vocal supporter of British engineering and manufacturing.

Then out of the blue, in February 2002, the company announced it was shutting its Malmesbury manufacturing plant with the loss of 590 jobs. It was moving the production of its upright cleaners to the Far East, where labour costs were much lower.

Everyone was amazed and appalled. Overnight the previously golden relationship that James Dyson and his firm had enjoyed with the media was seemingly wiped out. Phrases such as 'betrayal' and 'sell-out' were bandied about and acres of column inches were dedicated to deep soul-searching about the state of UK manufacturing, of which, until then, Dyson had seemed such a shining beacon.

Martin McCourt, Dyson's chief executive both then and now, explains the context for Dyson's decision:

> Big decisions like this usually come as a consequence of trying to solve big problems. Our problem was expansion. Our site was operating at full pelt, 24 hours a day, seven days a week and managing to output 1.5 million Dyson vacuum cleaners. But we needed more: we had designs on America, a bespoke product for Japan and orders from mainland Europe were really starting to come up.
>
> Obviously, we felt very attached to Malmesbury and the logical thing to do was to try to evolve from this point and seek solutions in our surrounding areas. We came up with some plans for some land beside the existing factory and had architect's models made of the supersized factories we'd need. It just so happened that Gordon Brown was visiting to open our new research and development centre, so we took the opportunity of all the local dignitaries being here to show them our plan for expansion. The reaction was dreadful. We immediately had a raft of both national and regional newspaper articles that basically said we were a blot on the landscape. They wrote, 'Are you not big enough?'
>
> We started to look at the problem in more detail and to think more about trends that we were already aware of, but hadn't really woken up to. A lot of our supply base, for example, was moving en masse to the Far East. So, we were procuring bits, bringing them all the way to Malmesbury, building the machines and then sending many of them back in that direction.

DECISION-MAKING LESSONS

› Follow your instincts, keep your head and don't panic, even if others around you don't want to go in the same direction.
› Be collegiate. Let everyone chime in with their view, but never take a committee approach to making the final decision.
› Hire exceptional people, light the flame and then let them get on with it.

Martin McCourt, Dyson

> We could also see that our suppliers were lowering costs and thought we could lower our costs by something like 40 per cent by manufacturing in the Far East.
>
> We were faced with a situation where our costs were going up, our margins were being compressed, our volume output was seriously challenged, and I was actually starting to introduce inefficiencies into the supply chain because I was fragmenting the UK manufacturing into anywhere I could find. It didn't make sense.

It's worth noting here that, as with so many big decisions, the basic problem was clear: Dyson was struggling with capacity and keeping its manufacturing competitive. To that extent the decision that had to be made was also a clear one: find a more competitive way to increase production. It wasn't a decision that could be parked. Dyson might have been performing well at the time, but everyone knew that it could fatally lose ground if it didn't address this fundamental issue. What turned the decision into a tough call, however, was the fury that everyone at Dyson knew our decision would unleash. We were fully aware that there would undoubtedly be a negative reaction from the media and the outside world at large. Internally, those who stood to lose their jobs would be very distressed, and those left behind would be suspicious and unsettled.

My view then, as now, was that the company had no choice but to move its manufacturing abroad if it wanted to take itself to the next stage of development, but I knew that it was virtually impossible to 'control' this highly emotive story. A right decision, however, doesn't become a wrong decision because it's not popular in all quarters. We opted to weather the storm and focus on executing the plan flawlessly. One thing we knew for sure: if James Dyson and his team were going to stand up and tell the world that the firm was moving its manufacturing to the Far East, they could not afford to muck up a single aspect of that move. The world would be watching. As Martin McCourt recalls:

> We knew that there would be a big reaction by the press and agreed that there was not a lot we could say. There was no point in James and I having extensive interviews trying to justify our actions, because it would never have changed the tone of the articles. We didn't feel that there was much we could protest about either because we were transferring to the Far East. The answer was to keep it quite simple and concise, making pretty much the same points as I've made here.
>
> Now, thanks to the passage of time, we can say more about it and people will listen. As a consequence of this transfer, we have been able to scale this business up from 1.5 million units to almost 6 million units in a space of a few years. In the process

our revenues have leapt from £200 million to over £900 million, heading towards a billion before too long. Therefore, if you look at the amount of tax that Dyson drops into Her Majesty's treasury, it is ten times more than it was back in 2002. Plus we now have 300 more people working at this site than we did at the peak of manufacturing.

We could have said this back then, but no one would have listened and I am not sure if it would have been the right pitch at the time anyway. We were better off in putting our energy into getting it right and proving everyone wrong.

Leadership is about 'Doing the Right Thing' – being able to look in the mirror each day and say to yourself that you really believe the decisions you are making are the right ones for the company's future. You can't hide a lie from yourself, nor can you indulge in a short-term popularity contest.

You need courage to do what James and Martin did, and courage is often in short supply. The big mistake many modern executives make is to believe that they can win a popularity contest if they avoid difficult decisions. It's tempting, of course. After all, we all want to be liked, and executives are surrounded by PR people anxious for good news and keen to avoid anything that might be problematic – there's always strong internal pressure to avoid controversy.

Equally tempting is to make the right tough call but then hold back when it comes to sharing it with the rest of the world. This, too, is a strategy that is asking for trouble. My view is that if you have made a major decision you have to have the confidence to handle it confidently and honestly. If you try to sugar the pill when talking about it to others you will fatally undermine it and you could end up with the worst of all possible worlds, appearing both weak and dishonest – not a good recipe for taking things forward.

My former colleague Archie Norman, who is now flexing his turnaround skills at ITV, believes with me that if you have the confidence to make a difficult decision, you have to follow through with the confidence to be straight about it. You can't undertake major surgery but pretend that you're really only changing the bandage and that everything will be back to normal shortly. Outsiders may be won over initially but will soon become sceptics when your bland and insincere promises don't immediately bear fruit. Insiders will start to assume that if those at the top aren't telling the truth, then they don't need to either and a climate of disinformation will start to build within the organisation. As Archie says:

> Instant change would be no change. Yet another false dawn. So we needed to ensure our shareholders provided the space for change. That meant being pretty brutal about the challenges we faced and where we were starting from. It meant presenting people with the 'unvarnished truth', our own people first and the shareholders and external media afterwards.
>
> It does not mean of course that you will make faster progress but it says you recognise the magnitude of the challenge.
>
> In our first set of results we stated that we operate in a flat declining market. Initially people – internally and even our brokers – thought this was a shocking thing to say. But television advertising revenue is today roughly the same as it was in 1999, so it is not a very contentious observation. And the market already knew it.

Once you tell the unvarnished truth, after years of defensiveness, the media and other commentators say, 'Ah I think they get it at last. This company, that has been pumping out the good news saying they are sailing on while their share price went down, never seemed to understand before. Now they get it.'

The long slog

The timetable for major decisions is a long one and involves several stages. There's that initial stage when you are absorbing information and deciding what to do. Generally speaking, this is something that ideally shouldn't be rushed, though it can't proceed at snail's pace either: you have to talk to people, to turn over ideas in your own mind and to formulate a plan. Then there's the execution phase, and after that comes the follow-through phase.

Whereas the initial planning stage may be flexible, execution and follow-through demand dynamism and constant activity. Sitting back and hoping that things will work out simply isn't an option. It's also essential to disprove the myth that big businesses are like super-tankers and that when the call comes down from the bridge that the company wants to swing round a few degrees it can take weeks, if not months, or even years, for the people down below to make the various adjustments to turn this big lumbering beast around. This to me is complete rubbish. Companies need pace. They need pace in decision-making and they need pace in making things happen. It shouldn't make any difference if there are a dozen people in the team or several thousand. If you get the culture right, when you want something to happen, it must happen, and fast. Speed and turnaround time give a competitive edge and develop the company muscles that are so necessary in tough times.

As BT chief executive Ian Livingstone puts it:

> **If you could do something that would personally save you a million pounds a year, you would do it today, right now, because if you did it next week it would have just cost you £20,000. In the corporate world, people often schedule a meeting for next week to talk about whether to take up that saving. Why wait? Pace is a really important thing.**

That doesn't mean that getting to your ultimate goal will be swift. When it comes to a major turnaround, you can be looking at a ten-year slog overall. Once you've decided on your strategy, the first six months will be spent fixing the major problems so that the company can survive. This is why the 100-day plan is a great catalyst in a tough call situation. It engages those at the top, galvanises the organisation, stretches the company's ambitions, and has a clear end date. The next three years involve renewing the organisation – bringing in new people as necessary, refining plans, setting a handful of more long-term goals. Years three to ten should be when you start to see a return on your initial decision-making, are able to set the pace for the next stage of development, and can see the culture of the company begin to develop. All three are linked, however, rather like a series of strokes in golf. Shots are not taken independently of each other – they all build towards a single target.

Culture, by the way, is a major aspect of a company's competitive edge. You can copy most things – products, systems – and quickly, too. But you can't copy culture because you can't see it. It's something in the DNA of the company. It has that 'cult' element to it which is what lies beyond some of the world's best companies. They have a language of their own and a 'business system' of their own, and it's the combination of the two that makes them unique. Customers today don't want sameness, they want uniqueness; and culture plus system equals uniqueness. Remember, too, that culture is a third what you inherit, a third what you put in, and a third pot luck, which is why it is so hard to define.

The human factor

One of the unpleasant but inevitable consequences of radical decision-making is that it often involves restructuring and, therefore, redundancies. Here I'm not talking about the 'internal terrorists' who are seeking to sabotage any change, but people who have often worked very hard for the company but whose role no longer fits with the direction the organisation is now taking.

Losing a job is a horrendous experience for anyone. It has huge implications emotionally, financially and domestically. Everyone knows this and, as a result, the tendency is for those in a position of power to put off the task of telling people that they no longer have a position at their firm. I've seen it happen time and again, particularly when a new broom comes in. They have all sorts of grand plans and yet they hesitate when it comes to implementing necessary cuts.

There are two options: 'fire early' or 'fire late'. Most people prefer the latter category, and that is almost invariably a mistake. Fire early really is the only call you can make if you want to do the right thing for your company.

There is no 'nice' way to make someone redundant. But it's actually worse if you hesitate than if you move swiftly. In my experience, unless they are particularly thick-skinned, or totally out of tune with their organisation, people generally know when they are under threat – whether because they are not doing a good job, or because their position effectively no longer exists, or because their department is drastically over-manned. They may pretend that they don't, but they do and every day they arrive at work is an agony of anticipation. They won't be able to concentrate because all they will think about from 9 till 5 is when the axe will fall.

Meanwhile, the people at the top cannot help but treat those who are earmarked to go differently. It is human nature. Mentally they have given up on them. At the back of everyone's minds is the knowledge that in all probability this person or that team won't be here in six months time, so there is little point telling them everything, or getting them involved in long-term projects. Day by day the basic tools that are needed for these people to do their job, such as information, are withdrawn. How would you feel?

In this difficult situation the best – and, actually, the kindest – thing you can do is to move swiftly. At the same time, you have to treat people with respect. One of the best pieces of advice I have been given when it comes to letting people go came from my old colleague at Mars, David Fish, now chairman of United Biscuits. He put it very simply: 'Fire people the way that you would like to be fired yourself.'

He is right. This advice counts for people at all levels of the organisation, from the junior warehouse person who only started in the job last month to a board director who may have been there for years. Everyone should be treated with equal respect and courtesy and feel that they have left a company with their dignity intact. Apart from the fact that this is a basic human right, the way that people are let go says everything about the company they worked for. Rest assured that ex-employees will always tell others about the way that they were fired, and if it was done badly word will get around.

The respect comes out in the way the redundancies are communicated. People should be told clearly and succinctly what is happening and why, and then be paid what they should be paid. Companies that try to save a few pennies by scrimping on redundancies always infuriate me. As part of the restructuring programme at Royal Mail we had to reduce the number of employees significantly. This involved moving 50,000 people out of the organisation over time, a decision that cost over a billion pounds. When government ministers expressed concerns to me about the scale and cost of the layoffs and the potential backlash from unions, my message to them was clear: we had to make people redundant to ensure the survival of the business, but the problems of the Royal Mail were not down to the people who were losing their jobs and therefore they must be paid adequate severance.

Chapter Two

The Crisis Decision

Imagine that you have just been parachuted into a highly successful company at a very senior level. Everything is fine when you arrive, but then the organisation is hit by a series of seismic shocks. Soon what was a very successful company is in crisis. Much of what is going wrong is clearly not your fault: key decisions may have been made long before you assumed a position of power. Nor does it seem that the organisation can really be blamed: so much of what is going on is down to external factors outside its control. What do you do?

The natural human instinct, of course, is to tell everyone who will listen that it's not your fault. That's fine as far as it goes, but it doesn't sort the problem and as the clock ticks while you make your excuses the problem grows and so does start to become your fault. Another fairly natural reaction is to blame others. Again, this doesn't get you very far and runs the danger of becoming a pointless distraction. Or you can say that the difficulties your company is experiencing are down to circumstances beyond its control.

That might fly for a day or two, but very swiftly your lack of action will be seen as contributing to the problem.

And if you think that all seems very unfair, consider the fate of some of those who got caught up in the banking crisis of 2007 and 2008. It may not be fashionable at the moment to defend bankers, but although some were clearly guilty of recklessness and worse, many who had acted responsibly were caught up in the maelstrom. And it came at breakneck speed. On 2 August 2007 three German banks revealed severe problems arising from their exposure to sub-prime loans. On 9 August BNP Paribas in France revealed that three of its investment funds were in trouble. On 10 August the FTSE-100 Index had its worst day in four years. On 14 August the financial authorities were alerted to the potential funding difficulties at Northern Rock. And that was just the first two weeks of the crisis.

In the months that followed, Northern Rock was to come close to collapse, Lehman Brothers was to fail and many high street banks were to lurch from one crisis to the next. HBOS alone experienced short-selling of its shares, rumours of Bank of England bail-outs, fears of a Northern Rock-style collapse, and an eventual takeover by Lloyds TSB.

Given the scale of the problem and the number of players involved, it would be absurd to say that one particular individual can be held responsible. Unfortunately, however, if you're in charge when things are going wrong around you, that doesn't really help. The person driving the car has to assume responsibility for swerving away from accidents and keeping it on the road. Entering a not guilty plea doesn't get you anywhere.

Immediate action required

When I talked about making radical decisions I pointed out that very often when there's a big internal problem it's not too difficult to identify what it is. The skill lies in formulating a plan and seeing it through. When you're making a crisis decision, things can seem very different. You're caught off guard. Everything seems to be happening at once. You can't control external events, nor can you make an accurate call as to what will happen next.

This volatility has certain implications. You don't have the luxury of being able to stand back while you decide what to do. Nor can you say that you will wait until all the facts are known – the chances are that by the time the facts are known it will be too late. In other words, you have to act straight away. But that doesn't mean a panic approach. In fact, to a very large extent, you need to adopt the same sort of mental rigour that you should apply to the radical decisions I have already discussed, but this time with the fog of war all around you.

The first thing is that there is no room for dithering when times get tough. One of the most demotivating things for everyone is when a leader can't make up their mind and gets swept along by events. If you're in a sinking ship, you don't want the captain to shout, 'Let's see what happens.' Indecision is unsettling. Constant indecision will invariably undermine the authority of the person at the top.

The second thing is that you have to avoid just that sort of mindset of denial that so often occurs in organisations in crisis. We witnessed a classic instance of this at Canadian retail giant Loblaw a while back. And, unlikely as it may sound, the crisis began with a mouse. Dalton Philips, then the COO at Loblaw, recalls:

A few years back we had a mice infestation in one of our stores, which is every retailer's nightmare. We were on the front page of the newspapers in Canada every day for five days and the share price was being hit. It was on my watch as COO, because I was in charge of all the shops.

It is not uncommon for mice to infiltrate a food-serving establishment, particularly in extreme cold weather with a rural spread of stores, but it is not a good situation and of course the store in question was immediately closed. Then, we got the call that we had a similar problem at a store on the West Coast. It was a really big deal now, with two stores closed, coast-to-coast and terrible national press comment.

DECISION-MAKING LESSONS
> Find a way to help the team continually hone their own decision-making skills, so they are ready when you really need them. That means giving them some leeway.
> It is about give and take. Every so often you have to let one through the gate because if you say no all the time it will screw the business up. You just have to make sure it is the right one. Create a culture where everyone is prepared to tell the truth. Without total transparency you will never have the right data on which to base your decisions.

Dalton Philips, Morrisons

When Dalton heard about the initial infestation, he immediately spoke to the store manager and district manager to find out what they were doing about it. 'Is this going to be a problem?' he asked. 'No, no, no,' they both said, 'it will be fine. We've seen the health inspector and we fully expect to get an OK in the morning.' What, of course, they should have said was, 'Yes, this is a serious problem. Let's assume the worst – that we won't be allowed to open tomorrow – and we'll do everything we can to fix things in the meantime.' You could say that they were being complacent, but the issue really was that they didn't want to have to engage with the potential ramifications of what was going on. They just wanted it to go away. In the morning the health inspector came around and, of course, shut the store down. Subsequently we took action against both members of staff, not because of the mouse, but because they had completely under-played the potential consequences.

A very different approach was adopted by Surinder Arora during the snow chaos that hit Heathrow Airport in December 2010, a crisis that affected him directly since one of his ever-growing network of hotels is the 605-bedroom Sofitel at Terminal 5. Of course, he could have argued that it was not his problem, or that the problem would go away in time, or that someone else should do something about it. Instead he bent his mind to the tens of thousands of passengers who were left stranded when the airport ground to a halt for several days before Christmas after heavy snowfall and freezing conditions iced up the runway and plane stands.

> **I came into the hotel at 9 o'clock and the queue of people wanting rooms was literally out of the door. If this was the situation at this time in the morning, all the hotels around Heathrow, not just my one, would be sold out in minutes.**

I said to my PA, 'Can you see if you can find me some sleeping bags? I need as many as you can get, maybe a few hundred?' She must have thought I had gone mad, but by about 11.30 am, she had found 500 sleeping bags out near Northampton thanks to the wonderful power of the Internet. However, as it was still snowing they needed an order by 2 o'clock to get them delivered that day.

I rang one of the directors at BAA and said, 'I have this crazy idea. You are not going to be able to get any hotel rooms because everything will be booked up. You don't want people sleeping on the floor in the terminals, but we can put them in our meeting rooms, in sleeping bags, feed them decent hot meals and let them use the shower facilities in the spa.' They said, 'Good idea, we will think about it.'

Two o'clock came and went and there was still no decision. I rang BAA again, reminded them of the deadline and they said they were still not sure.

I left my office at 5 o'clock to take my son sledging. The moment I pulled up at my front door I got a call from BAA saying, 'Can we take you up on that offer?' I really wasn't sure that I could get the bags by then as it was still snowing heavily. However, I said, 'Leave it with me.' I always try to fill my customers' requirements, so I asked Tommy, my gardener, if he could pick up 500 bags for me from Northampton in his van.

We had folks in sleeping bags in the hotel by 10 o'clock that night and some of them were with us for four or five days, because it was so bad. We opened up the theatre to show movie premieres, we turned a meeting room into an Internet café and had another kiddies' room with games and cartoons. We kept everyone occupied and they all loved it.

This is a classic example of a first-class decision-maker taking on a problem almost *before* it becomes their problem, coming up with a practical solution and implementing it. It may not have made the headlines, but Arora was one of the few organisations to come through the snow fiasco with its reputation unscathed, and there can be little doubt that a large number of grateful people will think of Arora next time they need a hotel. No wonder Surinder's hotel at Terminal 5 was voted the best airport hotel in Europe.

Sticking to first principles

The banking collapse shows – at its most extreme – the difficulties inherent in crisis decisions. Faced with a situation that changes from hour to hour – let alone day to day – with constant bad news coming in from outside, internal panic and external criticism, it's very easy to grab at possible solutions and lose sight of where you want to get to. But even at times like this there are certain things you absolutely have to keep in focus.

At the height of the financial crisis, in April 2008, HBOS made the very difficult decision to announce a £4 billion rights issue to bolster its ailing balance sheet. It also revealed a further £2.8 billion write-down on its credit investments. Neither decision could have been easy, but it was what was needed to repair the balance sheet battered by the global crunch. Months later, they were sitting across the table from their arch rivals at Lloyds TSB, discussing a previously unthinkable £12 billion deal. Lloyds, which then ranked fourth in the mortgage lending market with an 8 per cent share, was taking over HBOS, which had been the UK's biggest lender with a 20 per cent share.

What is clear is that those who struggled through the immediate crisis did so by focusing on the key issue: survival. All decisions had to be geared to that end, however unpalatable individual ones may have seemed. While others argued the rights and wrongs of individual cases and individual guilt, the impressive decision-makers screened out the extraneous white noise. Alan Greenspan, for example, was one who argued powerfully that this was not the time for playing a blame game or letting the 'guilty' go to the wall. 'You cannot calibrate liquidity to only rescue the deserving,' he pointed out.

The financial crisis was very tough indeed for bank leaders, but it was also tough for those not immediately in the eye of the storm. At Marks & Spencer, for example, Sir Stuart Rose could see an economic environment in which the markets were suffering and the country was clearly sliding into recession. This was a real concern for the retail giant he was running. In retailing, when times get tough, customers generally trade down. They may switch from their favourite brands to own-brand products, or even change store altogether to one that is perceived to be cheaper. The syndrome where shoppers divert from Waitrose to Sainsbury's, or Sainsbury's to Asda, or Tesco to Netto, is known as the 'Aldi effect'. It earned the moniker after the sudden boom in trade at discount stores at the start of the last downturn. For a company like Marks & Spencer, which has never sought to trade in the budget market, the risk that people might trade down was a major and potentially very damaging one.

On the surface, it seemed that Sir Stuart had a choice between two options. In food, he could ignore what was going on and hope that M&S would come through it all unscathed. Or he could substantially drop his prices to beat the 'Aldi effect'. What he actually did, though, was to devise a policy that stayed true to fundamental M&S principles. As he recalls:

> Our instant reaction was to recognise that people saw our foods as expensive and we could foresee a situation where everyone cascaded down to try different supermarkets. We made the strategic decision to take our margins down by £175 million a year in the belief that, over time, customers would recognise that we have got really good value and we would get that cash back.
>
> It worked. The best marketing thing we came up with, which was a huge success, was dining for £10. Everybody laughed to start with, but then every single person on the high street bar none copied it. That was our reaction to the downturn and we still maintained our quality standards. People didn't say they got nasty quality stuff. They said, 'Wow, I am getting M&S quality for £10. That is fantastic value.'
>
> We made sure that we were constantly re-establishing our core values. It was not about being price-driven, but being value-driven. We stuck to our guns. The last thing you should do is to try to be what you are not. It would have been insane for M&S to try to be like Primark or Tesco. M&S is not Primark or Tesco.
>
> You can build the margins back again, but it will take time. The most important thing is survival in a recession and keeping faith with your consumer.

This seems to me precisely the sort of decision-making you need here. Sir Stuart knew that doing nothing was not an option, but nor did he rush into making a decision that went against a formula that has made M&S so successful.

Keeping focus is something that I also sought to do at Loblaw during the financial crisis. We were already well stuck in to a massive shake-up, which included a major store renovation programme and installing one of the biggest retail supply IT systems ever. I had no doubt that Loblaw was one of the best super-market businesses in the world but I also knew that these changes were essential if we were to modernise.

With everything that was going on with the shake-up, it would have been tempting to try to ignore the economic downturn. I knew, however, that that would make us very vulnerable. The trick, then, was not to agree some completely new strategy aimed specifically at the financial crisis that might distract from what we were already trying to do but to focus on an approach that would complement the company overhaul.

I know from experience that in a recession cash is king – more an emperor than a king in this one – and so we turned our attention to what I called a 'cash marathon'. This involved intense scrutiny of every single way the business used cash, from capital, to receivables, to dividends, to inventory. It might seem a rather obvious thing to do, but in easy times the focus on cash lessens in most companies. My view, therefore, is that there is lots of loose cash that companies can get after. How much attention is really paid to levels of stock? When was the last time anyone really went through the terms a company has with its vendors in detail?

Nothing was sacred in the cash marathon. We looked at everything. And guess what we found: billions of dollars. In receivables we discovered we were far too generous in our payment terms and were in excess of the industry norms. Turning to our vast investment in capital projects, we targeted the team to negotiate up to a 15–20 per cent discount from every single vendor we worked with.

We carried this on all the way down the line and within six months had added significant cash to the balance sheet.

There is an immediate business lesson here: many companies in the boom years grew fat. People were just not focused on protecting cash in their business and thinking what they could do to make it work better. It was so simple to borrow money when we needed it, that everyone relaxed and took the easy way out.

Ian Cheshire, Kingfisher's chief executive, who took on the top job right at the start of the recession, did a similar housekeeping exercise at the DIY giant. His view is that those of us in the retail business were better equipped to deal with the fundamental shift in the economic world.

> Retailers are used to getting in every Monday morning and starting all over again. It is in our mindset. I'm sure that if you were running a 20-year-long oil field project, such massive economic shifts would have a devastating impact. It seems to me, though, that most retailers thought, 'Hmm, the world has changed, let's get on with it.' Everyone took on a trader's mentality and went hell for leather to get the cash in. As soon as we realised we couldn't rely on banks any more we immediately began looking elsewhere.
>
> Everyone was 'lucky' to some extent that there had been this build up of fat in our businesses. There was certainly a lot of unrealised potential in Kingfisher where it had become very decentralised through various acquisitions over time. This was a real opportunity for a big shake-up and to change the structure.
>
> We also created a bonus scheme for our top people which is something most retailers don't usually do. We told them that if they got their working capital sorted out they'd get a bonus.

Suddenly we generated an extra £700 million in cash and shareholders were asking why we hadn't done it before.

Having strengthened the balance sheet through the cash marathon at Loblaw, we also knew that our capital projects were producing better returns, that we had reduced our net debt, and that we were buying better. That's the point when we decided to invest more money into our capital programmes – in other words, use the fruits of the cash marathon to invest so as to ensure that we kept a competitive edge at a time of a market downturn. The object was a simple one: to come out of tough times stronger, not weaker.

DECISION-MAKING LESSONS
› There is a degree to which the perfect is the enemy of the good. If you wait for 100 per cent information and certainty before making a decision, you are definitely too late. If you make it on 20 per cent you are probably too early. It is about having the judgement.
› The data won't make the decision for you. You can analyse it in a million ways, but in the end you still have to make the decision.
› Listen to commentary and criticism from the outside, but never forget you know more about the business than they do.

Ian Cheshire, Kingfisher

It may not seem the most intuitive of strategies to consider, or the easiest to implement, but investing in a business in tough times can actually pay dividends. If you get it right, while others are pulling in their horns you can be pressing ahead of them. It's interesting to note, for example, how Sir Terry Leahy handled things at Tesco during the grimmest moments of the credit crunch:

> As a rule, when things are going well it is easier for everyone to do well. When things are difficult, the more determined, the stronger ones, get going. We have always made the most relative progress as a business in the more difficult times by keeping investing and upping the competition. If it is hard for us, it is really hard for others – indeed more than some others can cope with.
>
> This time, though, it didn't feel like an opportunity. The autumn of 2008, immediately post-Lehmans, was extraordinary for all businesses because for a moment no business could finance itself, or rely on its usual sources of finance. It didn't matter how big or profitable you were. Everyone immediately had to secure how they would finance themselves, which in our case meant we had to rely on cash flows from within the business. That is not how businesses operate. Yes, everyone has cash flow, but the normal sources of financing are equity, debt, asset sales and so on. We were used to a much wider pool of financing, which could be altered according to the cost and the availability. This was a massive change.
>
> Was it a 'great opportunity'? This time it was more like being in a marathon, gasping for breath when someone says, 'Let's put in a sprint; it will finish the other person off.' It is good in theory, but it doesn't feel great.

DECISION-MAKING LESSONS

› One of the hardest decisions is knowing how far you can push the business. The CEO always has to push the business farther than it wants to go itself.

› Businesses can recover tremendously from wrong decisions as long as they are not life-threatening. As long as you are not betting the company, you can take lots and lots of risks, and lots and lots of decisions, many of which go wrong and you'll still be fine.

› You learn more from the mistakes than from the successes, as long as you are honest and don't punish failure. Just say, 'Well that was a right lash up, let's have another go.'

Sir Terry Leahy, former CEO, Tesco

We kept investing once we secured our financing, though, and that has been good for Tesco. We did grow market share through the recession. 2009 felt good.

Sticking to core business values and disciplines in a crisis, then, may actually end up not just sustaining a company's fortunes, but enhancing them.

It's also important to remember that not all crisis decisions are about money. Good companies have a set of goals and aspirations that are not simply financially focused. These, too, need to be safe-guarded when crises rage.

Carolyn McCall, who came to easyJet from the Guardian Media Group in the summer of 2010, knew that she was joining an industry that is both famously unpredictable and famously prone to crises. In 2010 easyJet was hit by two: the drifting ash ejected from a volcano in Iceland that left millions of airline passengers around Europe stranded for a week and, just as Carolyn took up her post on 5 July, a period of what the tabloids love to call 'summer flight chaos' at easyJet. Just 48 per cent of the airline's planes were going out of Gatwick on time and hundreds of flights across all its routes were cancelled. The official line was that air traffic control services in Europe were to blame, but, as Carolyn quickly found out, easyJet had more flights scheduled than crew available. While there were a multitude of individual causes, including the knock-on effect of the ash crisis and air traffic control disruption, it was also clear that the company had stretched too few crew across too many flights.

She had various challenges on her hands:

It was easy to see what my priority was when I arrived. It was operations. I had to fix it very quickly and make sure we had enough crew, in the right place. In fairness, there had been a lot of people shouting about this internally for some time, but no one had listened to them before.

Then I had to build trust among the team, because a lot of people were very disheartened. I told them, 'Here is the plan, here are the actions I am taking now and here are the things we are working on for post-summer.' I then said, 'This is a great airline and it is a fantastic opportunity but we are only going to be able to deliver that if we are all in it together.'

However, she knew she couldn't afford to forget one fundamental value that cuts across all others:

> **The only thing that is absolutely black and white in this business is safety and we are one of the best airlines in the world on that. That is the only thing that can't change. On everything else, I am prepared to listen.**

Airlines may be an extreme example of this, but what they graphically demonstrate is how, when you're busily fending off problems left, right and centre, you can never afford to deviate from the core values that made your business successful in the first place.

I've always been impressed by the action taken by Jacques Nasser, the legendary Ford chief executive, when the car giant was hit by the so-called 'tyre crisis' at the end of the 1990s, involving rollover incidents among Ford's flagship four-wheel drive Explorer sports utility vehicles.

First Jacques took immediate practical steps, involving a product recall and an invitation to Explorer owners to visit dealers to change affected tyres. As he recalls:

> **It was one of those times where a decision had to be taken quickly; that decision was clear and then a multiple number of follow on decisions were required in terms of how to implement it.**

Then he set out half a dozen key principles for everyone in his company to follow, arguing that without these the company would be left like 'a cork bobbing in the ocean', constantly reacting to the latest headline or political statement

Of course, top of the list was that we would do everything possible to enhance the safety of our customers. We also had to protect the long-term reputation of the company.

If we hadn't set out these principles it would have been easy to be swayed off course in every subsequent decision we made.

At times like this, things will change. They will change every day. But, if you have set out the principles that must be followed, then you provide clarity and simplicity to the team. No one in the organisation will be in doubt as long as they go back and test every decision against these principles.

We didn't just set out the principles and say, 'Ok we all know them now; let's just get on with putting things right.' We constantly went back to them, time and again. I did not stop communicating them to the team.

DECISION-MAKING LESSONS

› Gather the facts and be as fact-based as you possibly can, but in the end you have to trust your own judgement.
› Anyone who says they haven't made mistakes in decision-making probably hasn't done very much.
› The toughest choices are when there is not any clear answer, or when the alternatives are really close. With all the others you decide on a course of action, bring your people with you and focus on implementation.

Jacques Nasser, BHP Billiton

Calling the toss

So far I've talked about keeping focused on the big picture and making sure that you don't rush into doing things that might actually run counter to what made your business successful in the first place. That famous line from the TV cult classic *Dad's Army* – 'Don't panic, Captain Mainwaring!' – is always on my mind. The danger is, though, that with a broader range of decisions now to make – both the everyday ones and the ones designed to cope with the crisis – you start making some bad calls. How do you avoid that?

The answer, I believe, is to stand back for a moment every time you need to make a decision and ask yourself two questions. What's the worst that can happen if I take this course of action? And what's the best that can happen? It may sound very obvious, but it can be an extraordinarily useful mental exercise.

A classic and extreme example that demonstrates the power of this came during the Kosovo War in 1999, when General Sir Mike Jackson famously refused to obey an order from American General Wesley Clark, his immediate superior in the NATO chain of command, to take Priština airport on the grounds that the Russians, who had played a crucial role in persuading Yugoslav President Slobodan Milosevic to end hostilities, were already occupying it. General Sir Mike vividly recalls that day:

> Time was extraordinarily short on that occasion. We had about three hours from the situation arising to thinking, 'What the hell are we going to do?' Having quickly run through with my planning staff that our understanding of the situation was common, otherwise you would get different answers from

different understandings, we all went our separate ways for an hour to do our mission analysis.

Mission analysis is a rather pompous way of saying, 'What is it we are required to do?' The tool to do this is very simple. It is three little words: ends, ways and means.

The end is: what is it they want of me? Or, where do I want to be? It is like a journey. You know where you are and you have to define where you want to be at the end.

Then, you have to have some means. Means are the people who you lead, money, machines and even time, because time is also a means.

The art of leadership is the *way* in which means are applied in order to achieve the end.

From this analysis of what it is you are setting out to do, you will almost certainly deduce a number of different approaches and each will have their advantages and disadvantages that have to be weighed up.

Then, at some point, the debate will stop. You will have to make the decision.

Actually, in this case, the decision was quite easy. When I met up again with my planning staff an hour later, we all felt that what we were being asked to do was nonsensical.

If we had gone ahead, we could have finished up with x number of dead or wounded British and Russian soldiers lying around this relatively unimportant little Balkan airfield. That would have been the lid of Pandora's Box. We were only a few years out of the Cold War and the risk–benefit equation of what I was being asked to do simply didn't work.

DECISION-MAKING LESSONS

› It is always sensible to listen to that little voice at the back of your head that says, 'Are you quite sure that you have not got this wrong?' Check, check, check.

› I worry about it when people are absolutely obstinate about a decision and won't move an inch. Very few issues can be reduced to such black and white terms that it is worth digging such a big hole over.

› We may have every electronic aid to communication to get decisions down the line, but there is something about the human condition that means you can take the horse to water, but you can't always make it drink. You have to work hard at communication and do as much as humanly possible face-to-face.

General Sir Mike Jackson

It's a classic example of cool-headed decision-making under pressure – and both then and in retrospect it was clearly the right decision to make. If you apply the 'Best that could happen/Worst that could happen' rule, you get a very uneven result. The best that could have happened was that General Sir Mike would have won General Clark's approval and that British and American troops would have occupied a particular airfield. The worst that could have happened was a total breakdown in relations with the Russians and dead British and American troops. Analysed like that, the initial decision simply didn't stack up. As General Sir Mike said to General Clark after a very heated exchange: 'I'm not going to start the Third World War for you.'

During the banking crisis all those in the banking industry were forced to analyse nearly every decision in terms of what was the worst that could happen. In their case the worst case scenario was that there could be a run on the banks and the entire industry could implode. Anything that could be done to avoid that clearly made sense, however unpalatable the individual decision.

Learning to anticipate

Good leaders and decision-makers are often slightly paranoid. Only the paranoid survive. They are always looking ahead, trying to predict what might go wrong even if things happen to be going really well at that moment. But, of course, predicting every eventuality is impossible. Carolyn McCall is only too aware of this in the airline industry:

> With an airline there are so many unknowns. Early on in the job, I asked [BA boss] Willie Walsh if he had the volcano on his risk map. 'You have to be joking,' he said. Nobody talked about volcanoes at that time. Then it came out of the blue and grounded airlines. Twin Towers was the same. No one expected that. So, these are the unknown unknowns.

Then there is the oil price, which everyone can forecast and hedge, but could anyone have definitely said that the price of oil was going through the roof for a sustained period of time? That is more of a known unknown.

So you have unknown unknowns and you have known unknowns. That makes it very challenging when you are trying to make plans for the future.

The fact that some things are tough to predict, though, doesn't mean that you can afford to be complacent about them. After all, by its very nature, the unlikely will occur at some point – as Nassim Taleb pointed out in his influential book, *The Black Swan*. And if unlikely events are, by their very nature, difficult to spot, that should increase the sense of paranoia that good leaders so often have – the determination to look ahead and see what might go wrong.

Accepting that the unlikely may well occur could help highlight a potential problem ahead. Failing that, it will create a mindset adaptable enough to cope with the unpredictable.

Chapter Three

The Opportunity Decision

It was the spring of 2008 and the global financial crisis was at its height. In the UK, Northern Rock, which had started to fall apart the previous autumn, was taken into state ownership. In France BNP Paribas, the country's biggest listed bank, briefly suspended customer withdrawals. In the US, the collapse of the $2 trillion subprime market was starting to pull down banks with it. Bear Stearns, one of the country's Big Five, was rescued at the eleventh hour by JP Morgan on 25 March. Now Lehman Brothers was starting to look distinctly wobbly.

Lehman's difficulties now became Barclays' opportunity. We all know that frantic last-minute deals were being negotiated before the bank finally collapsed in September. What is not widely known, though, is that Barclays started to look at Lehman several months before.

It is worth exploring Barclays' deliberations about Lehman in some detail, because they offer a textbook example of how decision-making should work when a potentially massive opportunity comes your way.

The first step along the way came in the early summer of 2008 when Barclays was first sounded out about the possibility of a rescue deal. At that time, those in authority in the US had a pretty fair idea that the early financial casualties might not be the last and had begun to stress test a series of 'unthinkable' scenarios. Earlier, US Federal Reserve President Timothy Geithner had stopped Bear Stearns folding completely by creating a $29 billion bailout to encourage JP Morgan to assume the firm's obligations. Now, with one eye on the next most vulnerable bank, Lehman Brothers, Geithner and Treasury Secretary Henry 'Hank' Paulson began quietly to cast their net for another JP Morgan-style rescue deal.

Marcus Agius, Barclays' chairman, described to me how Barclays became involved:

> They phoned up everyone who they thought might be capable of acting in JP Morgan's role and naturally the call came in here too. They called Bob Diamond [then chief executive of Barclays Capital] and the question that was asked was, 'Is there any price at which you could be interested in buying Lehman Brothers?' Bob, very properly, gave them an equivocal answer. He didn't say yes and didn't say no. He just sort of logged it. In fact, the question came through more than once.

John Varley, Barclays' group chief executive, became involved and he and Bob Diamond together with their top advisers got together to scrutinise a potential deal and to discuss the upsides and the downsides. The upsides promised to be considerable. As Marcus recalls:

The core business was fantastic. We were very keen to increase our business in America and history shows that to do that organically is very difficult, so if we could buy a good asset that would be a good thing to do. These deals are as rare as hens' teeth, so we owed it to ourselves to think about it.

Here, then, were two factors in the deal's favour: not just an opportunity to buy a fundamentally good business, but to buy one that would help fulfil a long-cherished Barclays goal. On the other hand, it was equally clear that Lehman was loaded down with toxic assets that could well infect a buyer. And Barclays were anxious to avoid getting into an auction for the business because, as Marcus says, 'we had just lost out on a bid for ABN Amro and to lose two auctions in a row is not a good thing'.

Next Barclays called an exceptional board meeting in July to focus exclusively on the Lehman opportunity:

A board briefing paper was produced and we chewed it over very thoroughly for two or three hours. All the right questions were asked. The sense of due enquiry happened. Everyone on the board was involved, asking, 'What about this? What about that? How do we know about this? How do you know about that? What is the consequence of this? What risk is involved in that?'

It wasn't a mainstream decision, it was an opportunistic thing. Therefore the debate took place in an atmosphere where there was no need for and no occurrence of aggression or hostility from the non-executives. They were genuinely asking the right questions for the right reasons. If they asked a sensible question, they got a sensible answer. Well, the best answer we could give, anyway.

At the end of the process, we ran out of questions and summed up.

The Barclays board reached a series of conclusions: first that they were definitely interested in Lehman Brothers; secondly that under no circumstances would they buy the bank if they had to inherit its toxic assets; thirdly that the price had to be so low as to be irresistible; and fourthly that they would not get into an auction situation.

At the end of the meeting, John Varley thanked everybody and said he thought it had been a useful discussion. He added that he had to manage expectations and that the chances of it happening were as close to zero as makes no difference. But we had owed it to ourselves to examine it. Then we didn't think about it very much.

That's how things rested until the weekend of 13 and 14 September. As the financial world teetered on the edge, Hank Paulson convened an extraordinary Saturday meeting with Wall Street chiefs in the fortress-like headquarters of the New York Federal Reserve. Although Lehman was on the brink of collapse, there would be no bailout for the 160-year old investment bank, he told the bank bosses. They must consider pooling resources to set up a 'bad bank' to buy up toxic assets, so Lehman had some chance of being sold. He added that unless they acted, the financial system of America, and the world, would meltdown in a matter of days.

As the clock ticked, Barclays started receiving calls from New York. Presented with the opportunity again, but this time with added urgency, Barclays didn't shift from their previous carefully considered stance:

> We had our little box which said what we needed to be able to deal with it. We stuck to our conditions that the price would have to be very low and it would have been very low because the share price was almost nothing at that stage. Also, we said, 'No toxic assets.' Remarkably, on the Saturday, Hank Paulson had dragooned the Wall Street bosses and got them to agree to fund a bad bank. So we could have bought it 'clean'. As far as the auction was concerned, Bank of America, who had been in the running to buy Lehman, decided on Saturday to buy Merrill Lynch. So we had a clear run at it.

As everyone knows, that particular deal fell apart at the last moment because Barclays would have to have had a shareholder vote before it could buy Lehman and there was clearly no time for such action; failing that, the US government would have had to guarantee Lehman's liabilities until such a vote could be properly convened, but such a guarantee was declined.

DECISION-MAKING LESSONS
› Surround yourself with clever people who know how to do good things.
› Good decisions require everyone to be totally familiar with the facts and that means complete honesty and transparency from the top.

Marcus Agius, Barclays

Inevitably, on 15 September, Lehman was forced to file for Chapter 11 bankruptcy protection. However, the following day Barclays announced that, subject to regulatory approval, it would be purchasing Lehman's trading and investment banking operations in North America, as well as its headquarters in New York, from the liquidator.

Looking back on this period of frantic activity – and in particular the debates that occurred over the weekend of 13/14 September – Marcus concludes:

> The presumption on the outside is that we would have done this mad thing based on a few hours' deliberations. Well we weren't mad at all. It was very precisely delineated and we would only have done it had we got those conditions which we had carefully set out at that earlier meeting.

This is textbook decision-making, and so it's worth looking at the key moments along the way in a little more detail.

Take your time, keep your cool

The first thing to note about Barclays' approach is that they didn't rush things. There was that initial moment when the potential deal was mentioned, then a period when internal discussions were held, culminating in a lengthy board meeting. It was only at this point that Barclays made their offer. Such a measured process allowed the key players to establish what the benefits and the risks were. (As I mentioned before, it's always a good idea to ask yourself when faced with one or a series of possible strategic decisions, 'What's the best that could happen or the worst that could occur?') It also gave them time to do the best due diligence that they could.

Studying the evidence before your eyes seems such an obvious thing to do that you might think it doesn't need to be mentioned. But it's extraordinary how often careful consideration of the facts collapses in the face of the excitement that a sudden opportunity can give rise to. Faced with something big and ambitious, people have a tendency to throw caution to the wind, exchanging a cool, rational approach for an excited 'What if?' attitude. Optimistic forecasts all too easily overcome present realities, as News Corp's James Murdoch argues:

DECISION-MAKING LESSONS
› It is hard to make a hierarchy of decisions. Some that seem hard now may turn out as of little importance later on. Others that seem easy now can turn out to be a real headache further down the line. That is why you really need to think them through carefully.
› Once you are committed, and the bell goes, you are in for the round. You can't climb out of the ring in the middle.

James Murdoch, News Corp

Evidence is often underrated, particularly in the UK. People come to me with all sorts of models of the future that are supposed to help me make decisions. I often hear people talking about models that show X, Y and Z and arguing that there could be better outcomes if this or that or the other happens. I would always rather look at the history and deeply understand the here and now, as opposed to an economist's model going forward.

Of course, time isn't always on your side. Opportunities by their very nature are unexpected and the timeframe involved can vary wildly. Sir Martin Sorrell, whose relentless deal-making at WPP has transformed it from a shell-company into the globe's largest advertising group, believes strongly in being able to turn on a sixpence, and believes that swift decision-making can be a real virtue:

> If you talk to our advisers, they would say that our greatest strength in deal situations is being able to make rapid, rapid decisions, whereas what usually happens in most companies is it takes them too long to make decisions. Companies get bogged down in bureaucracy, or legal arguments or complex financial instruments, particularly when a bid is contested or hostile. This doesn't just work well for us in the context of takeovers; it has also served us well in day-to-day decisions. We are very different to many other companies in that respect.

But there's an important proviso to be made here. What Sir Martin is criticising is that institutional inertia that so often slows down big, unwieldy companies. You can still ask and seek to answer the right questions whatever the timeframe involved is. Mental discipline is everything.

DECISION-MAKING LESSONS

› A bad decision on Monday is better than a good decision on Friday.
› All businesses are about geography and technology at the end of the day. A leader just has to think about how the business is changing and try to make the decisions that will get the business in the right place.
› Leading a company and making all the decisions that go with that is not a job, it is fun. There is no such thing as stress. Stress just means that you are not enjoying yourself.

Sir Martin Sorrell, WPP

This kind of mental discipline – the stripping down of issues into their component parts – works well, too, when you're seeking to grapple with several apparently disparate choices at once. It happens all the time. It's like the old cliché about buses: there isn't one for ages and then three come along at once. You've just got to decide which one is the best one to catch.

Another good example of this is the series of major decisions faced by Ian Cheshire when he joined giant Kingfisher in January 2008. He had an excellent track record, having sorted out Kingfisher's hotchpotch of international businesses over the previous three years and presiding over a 16-fold rise in profits in the foreign interests. But he faced a number of issues. The international part of Kingfisher might have been doing well, but the rest of the business was in dire straits, with £1.8 billion of debt and very little cash generation. There were rumours of a potential break-up bid. Moreover, he took over just as the world financial crisis was reaching its peak.

Into this unwelcome mix came two opportunities: the possibility of selling off Kingfisher's Screwfix online business or selling the Castorama DIY retailer in Italy. Either would help the balance sheet. The downside was that announcing a sale that then, for some reason or other, didn't come off could undermine the CEO – or, as Ian put it, make him look 'a total prat'. However, to that extent both strategies were equal. What Ian had to do was to decide which one had the edge:

> I had to decide which was the riskier one to sell. Which bit could we get more for, as part of a bidding competition? I also had to consider the whole regulatory bit, as to which one would get a quicker completion rather being embroiled in an extended anti-competition enquiry. The aim is to end up with a very finely judged decision.

Eventually, he made his decision:

> I persuaded the board that we should sell the Italian business because we were number three in Italy and were probably never going to be number one; plus we had two potential bidders who would compete for the asset. As it was it was a very lengthy process. In the end we got the deal through just weeks before Lehman went bust in October. If we had started the process any later we would have been stuffed.

Ian was vindicated in his plan and profits at Kingfisher have grown steadily since he took the helm, despite challenging conditions for the DIY market during the credit crisis.

If you look at the problems and opportunities facing Ian here all together they seem almost impossibly complex. You've just taken over a business in crisis. You need to be seen to be doing something, but you can't afford to make a mistake with your first big decision. A financial meltdown is going on around you which is making credit tight and scrutiny of your company tighter still. You have options that range from cutting costs to selling off two very different businesses. But, as always, Harold Macmillan's belief that 'Calm deliberation untangles every knot' works here. First you stand back and consider your options, then you drill into each one forensically. In the case of Kingfisher bewildering choice and priorities were reduced to one well-executed decision.

Such coolness and careful consideration is a hallmark of Sir Terry Leahy, one of the foremost business leaders of our time who during his time at Tesco bought and sold a fair few companies. His rules are clear and simple:

> Deals have to be done in a calm and detached way. You've always got to be able to say 'no'.
>
> The big thing for me at Tesco is: I never bet the company. That puts acquisitions in a slightly different strategic order. Anyone who spends anywhere north of 30 per cent of the value of their company on an acquisition is close to betting the company. If it goes well it is fantastic, but if it goes wrong they are wiped out.
>
> This, of course, means that you can't use a big acquisition to get the long-term growth, so all growth has to be essentially organic. But, as our acquisitions were never more than 10 per

cent of the business, they quite quickly fell into the relatively ordered process about how we looked at the company. We were calm enough to take time to see how it fitted and look at the execution process, the real value and so on. It makes it a much more logical approach. It has to be cold-blooded. If you make it subjective then it can get very unpredictable.

It's always good to have certain iron rules that you're not going to break. It's particularly important when something apparently exciting comes along because the chances are that many people are going to get caught up in the excitement of the moment. In merger talks, for example, those on one side will be desperate to be seen to be pulling off some great coup; those on the other will be trying to ramp things up, suggesting that at least two or three other parties are sniffing around and that time is of the essence. Sir Terry copes with this by having in mind a percentage of the company's value beyond which he won't go. I deal with it similarly by applying my own golden rules to keep things in perspective at times like this.

First, and most importantly, there has to be a 'fit', both in the cultures of the companies and among the individual personalities. They don't have to be exactly the same, in fact that is pretty unlikely, but if you can't imagine everyone getting on when they are in the same room together, it is probably not going to work.

Secondly, look carefully at any supposed synergy savings that could be made by merging offices, or operations and the like, and then discount the benefit of these synergies by 30 per cent. (I always add in the costs of putting at least three of my top management team into the merged business too). Then make a rough calculation of how long it is all going to take. The most important part of this exercise is: if you can see that it is going to take a long time to deliver any of these synergy benefits, then don't do it. To me, a 'long time' is anything more than two years. The longer something takes, the more chance there is that something can go wrong. As time goes on, everything just ends up costing more and you will get less out of the deal.

These sorts of iron rules provide discipline and keep you focused. It's a bit like an auction situation. There's something you desperately want to buy, but if you're prudent you will set yourself a limit before you cross the threshold of the auction house. If you're imprudent you will allow yourself to get swept up in the hysteria of the moment – and you will almost invariably overpay. Remember: it's rare to suffer because you've made a decision not to buy something; it's an inevitability that you will suffer if you've overpaid. Having a benchmark in mind – and, ideally, a clear view of the potential downside – is crucial.

Talk to others

When faced with a major opportunity no decision can be made without discussion with others. There are two simple reasons for this. One: if you've got good people around you, you need their brains. Two: if you make a decision that lies outside everyday management, you need others to buy in. They might not all necessarily agree, but consultation first ensures a collegiate attitude later.

This is clearly what happened at Barclays during the Lehman debate, and it's what all good decision-makers do. Sir Stuart Rose, who has been through numerous takeover, merger and hostile bid situations, is an excellent example. In 1997, as chief executive of Argos, he defended the company from a hostile bid from catalogue retailer GUS. In his next job, leading the Booker wholesale operation, he oversaw the merger with Iceland to form the Big Food Group. Then, in 2002, after rejoining Arcadia, he sold the group for £800 million to Sir Philip Green, only to lock horns again with Sir Philip a few years later, when as chief executive of Marks & Spencer he successfully fought off a high-profile bid from the retail tycoon. Such experiences have forcefully brought home to him just how much you need good advice when a major opportunity comes along:

> **In a bid situation you absolutely have to get the best people in with the requisite skills and let them have their say. If you have the best lawyer, let the best lawyer give his opinion. If you've got the best investor relations communicator, let him or her have their view. Listen to what they have to say. Don't invite all these people in and ignore their advice.**
>
> **What I know is mostly about shop-keeping. There is not much the best lawyer in town can teach me about shop-keeping. There is not much the best communicator can teach me about shop-keeping either. I can't do finance though, so I get the best banker.**
>
> **In a bid situation, leaders have to be able to distil the issues down to the essentials and cut out all the extraneous background noise. You need good people to help you with that.**

Of course, that means you need to surround yourself with people you can trust – something I will return to later. For the moment, it's just worth bearing in mind Sir Stuart's view on teams.

> The biggest failure of leadership is those managers who lack confidence so they surround themselves with bad or indifferent people because they think everyone is out to nick their job. If someone wants my job, I think it's great. It keeps me sharp and it will keep him sharp too. There is nothing wrong with that. If you are insecure you shouldn't be a leader.

It's important to remember, though, that discussion doesn't mean delegation of authority. Ultimately, it's still down to the person in charge to make the call. As James Murdoch says:

> Crucially, you have to remember whose responsibility it is to make these decisions. You may be given comfort by all the people around you but, ultimately, you have to be accountable. Sometimes you have to call time on all of those inputs and just say, 'I need to go away and consider this. I will make the decision myself in my own time and get it done then.'

Don't allow opportunity to blow you off course

There is a very important distinction to be made between grabbing an opportunity and being opportunistic. When Barclays were agonising about Lehman they knew that at the heart of everything was a great opportunity: the possibility of acquiring a major player in the US market where Barclays had long wanted to have a presence. They didn't base their thinking on an opportunistic desire to grab a large company just because it happened to be on offer.

This is a crucial discipline and one that is all too often forgotten, particularly in the heat of battle. It's the discipline that stops you saying yes when all the evidence is pointing to no, and vice versa. Charles Dunstone, who is no stranger to buying and selling businesses, is a business leader I particularly admire because he is so ruthlessly self-controlled when it comes to considering potential deals. Over the years the company Charles founded, Carphone Warehouse, has bought numerous small companies, including Tandy, Cellcom and Xtra. He has also notched up many bigger deals too, such as buying the UK businesses from both AOL in the US and Italian telecom group Tiscali, as well as selling a 50 per cent share of his company to US giant Best Buy. But if you think this means that he would buy anything that came up, you would be very wrong:

> You have to be disciplined, know what a business is worth to you and not get consumed by bidding fever. We were thrown out of the bidding process for Tiscali twice for not offering enough, but we bided our time. The first time we put in an offer in the range of £800 million to £1 billion and they didn't even bother to let us know that we hadn't made it to the next round. By the time the deal they had in mind collapsed, the world had changed, so we bid in a range from £450 to £600 million. They threw us out again. In the end, after all this, we bought it for about £210 million because we knew our price and just stuck at it. If someone else had paid a whole load more money, so be it because it was their money to spend. We are never going to overpay and jeopardise our business because we know how hard it has been to make what we have got.

DECISION-MAKING LESSONS

› If you have something that doesn't seem immediately solvable, just park it in your brain for a few days and stop worrying about it. Quite often it will all become clear and you will wonder why you struggled.

› Don't overcomplicate decisions by analysing everything in too much detail. The more straightforward and uncomplicated a problem is, the easier it is to solve.

Charles Dunstone, Carphone Warehouse,
Talk Talk

Asda in the early days of recovery was a company that was reeling from its inability to walk away from the wrong opportunities. In the 1970s and 80s it made a series of acquisitions, such as the Wades and Allied Retailers chains, which both sold carpets and furniture. Then in 1985 it merged with MFI, well known for its flat-pack, self-assembly kitchens. The reason given at the time was that these all presented great opportunities that took Asda outside the narrow grocery business where there was limited growth potential. Of course, you can convince yourself of anything, but the fact was that it was the grocery business that had made Asda successful, not carpets, furniture or kitchens. These may have seemed like opportunities, but actually they were dangerous distractions. The Asda management had little experience of managing non-food outlets and it was what was bolted onto Asda rather than its core business that ultimately threatened to pull it down.

In my own time at Asda there were plenty of opportunities that we didn't go ahead with. We looked at buying Kwik Save but decided not to, largely because we were not sure that Kwik Save was going to survive. The chain was being attacked on all sides by other supermarkets and just didn't have its original edge as a discounter any more. It sounds brutal, but we decided that the best thing to do would be to trade it out of existence, and I don't think I was the only grocery CEO to think this way. Indeed, given the chain's subsequent problems (it went into administration in July 2007, after several turbulent years), that proved to be the right decision.

We also considered hooking up with the Safeway supermarket chain in a number of different ways, but could never get the deal done, partly because we would have had to get rid of many stores to satisfy competition rules and also because we could never agree on the terms of the deal. At one time we wondered whether to take on the Welcome Break motorway service station business – after all, we already had experience in petrol and convenience retailing and the 'Asda price' low price position lent itself perfectly to budget hotel rooms. However, that deal threatened to be too expensive and we made the decision to walk away.

Eventually, two opportunities came along at almost the same time. In 1999 Archie Norman and I entered merger talks with Kingfisher. And just as these talks were reaching an advanced stage, Walmart let it be known that they might be interested in doing a deal too.

Archie and I had a lot to talk about. The thinking around the original deal with Kingfisher was sound. Kingfisher then owned the Woolworths variety store, Superdrug the chemist, UK home improvement giant B&Q and such continental DIY chains as Castorama and Brico Depot. So, here was a group that was great at general merchandise, but didn't sell food. Asda, on the other hand, was pretty good at selling food, but was really keen to beef up its general merchandise offering. If you got into the nitty gritty of it all, it sounded even more attractive. Asda's George clothing brand was at that time still pretty small, but we had high ambitions for it. By linking up with Woolworths, which had the Ladybird childrenswear range but little else by way of clothing, we could get George out to literally hundreds of high-street stores at a stroke. Similarly, although we had a reasonably sized pharmacy business, linking up with Superdrug would take us into a whole new arena. Then there were the obvious synergies, such as closing either the Kingfisher or Asda head office.

In fact, if you scrutinised the deal like this, it all looked pretty good. Plus, in its favour, there were very few unknowns because we knew the business well. The only parts of it we didn't really know about were the continental DIY chains, but we didn't see that as a deal-breaker.

There was just one problem though. As the talks progressed with Kingfisher, I began to realise that if we went ahead with a deal I would be breaking one of my golden rules: don't mate with what you hate. Our people kept returning from meetings with Kingfisher and saying, 'We are not going to get along with these guys. They seem to have a completely different way of doing business.' We'd send one or two people along for the meetings, while they would fill the room full of advisers. We were used to a culture of moving fast and getting things done; the talks with Kingfisher, however, seemed to be moving at a glacial pace. This was hardly surprising given all those people putting in their two pennyworth.

Then, along came Walmart. Weighing up the deal on a similar

basis, the US company had a lot in its favour. Walmart is, after all, the biggest buyer of general merchandise in the world, so if Asda's intention was to beef up its general merchandise, this deal was a no-brainer. It would give us a buying scale beyond our wildest dreams.

Any deal would be a straight cash transaction too, with Walmart buying Asda outright. That was potentially far more attractive than a complex merger agreement with Kingfisher. It would certainly be great news for our shareholders.

Finally, and most importantly, there was a cultural fit. After all, we had modelled much of Asda's culture on that of Walmart, which I had studied obsessively over the years. It was scarcely surprising that when I spoke to the Walmart directors I felt we were all speaking the same language.

The deal with Walmart was negotiated, signed, sealed and delivered within a week.

I often wonder what would have happened had Asda pursued the merger with Kingfisher. The fortunes of our erstwhile suitor certainly changed in the years following our failed discussions. In 2001, Kingfisher was forced into the sale and demerger of various parts of the company, including Woolworths, which became the Woolworths Group, and later on the electrical businesses that became Kesa Electricals. I am not sure things would have turned out much better had our two companies got together. Apart from the drag on our business that Woolworths and Comet would have imposed, there was that whole issue of the lack of a good cultural fit.

The Kingfisher deal may not have happened, but there is no doubt that the experience that I gained from the long and convoluted discussions I had with them, along with other negotiations I have had in the course of my career, paid dividends. It helped me hone my understanding and skills, and helps to explain why I now feel more able, like many other business leaders, to make swift decisions when opportunities arise. It's not about being any less forensic in approach; it's that experience has helped to give me a sixth sense of what will work and what won't – it's that 'intuition' mentioned earlier.

Gail Rebuck, CEO of the publishers Random House, nicely encapsulates what lies behind a successful decision-maker's intuition:

> People often talk about the use of intuition in making business decisions – the gut feel that some leaders refer to as an almost mystical ability, so somewhat daunting to those who do not feel they have it and probably not one that could be easily taught. Tough decisions are taken on the basis of careful analysis and lots of debate. However, the most senior person in the team eventually has to say yes or no and it can often be a narrow choice.
>
> When intuition or gut feel comes into play for me, I suspect my mind is unconsciously processing years of experience out of which an instinct for the right decision emerges. I have likened it to a microprocessor in the brain categorising and testing all the arguments until a way forward is found. I can also have an intuition about a new direction for the company or a department in difficulty which again probably comes as a result of hearing a series of faint signals carefully stored which, in aggregate, point to an opportunity or a problem.
>
> I often give advice to young people and tell them to follow their instincts. They may fail, but at least they will learn from failure. Learning to trust your instincts, which are honed over years of experience, is a core part of being able to make effective, tough decisions.

Never get out of one hole by digging another

They say, 'Never look a gift horse in the mouth', but it's worth remembering that there aren't actually many gift horses around. There are certainly plenty of opportunities, but that's not the same thing.

Consider takeovers and mergers, for example. It's very easy to think that by taking over another company or merging with it you can do all sorts of clever things to realise its value. How many times have you seen a wonderfully upbeat announcement about some new union of companies where you're told that this move will solve at a stroke the problem with skills or expertise one company was experiencing, or will result in greater synergies and buying power, or will improve productivity, or will make the new entity market leader? Would they really be improved? Well, possibly. But actually, most companies are already pretty good, and it's fatal to exaggerate the benefits that can be achieved. That alone serves to explain why so many apparently brilliant takeovers and mergers prove to be nothing of the kind.

This is particularly the case when people desperately seize an opportunity that comes their way in the hope that it will sort out an existing problem. In my experience, this almost never happens. Opportunities should be grabbed when they offer the possibility of making an existing situation better. They should definitely be regarded with suspicion if the people seizing them are in trouble themselves.

Adam Crozier, formerly chief executive of the Football Association and Royal Mail, regards this as the mythical silver bullet phenomenon, and he has had first-hand experience of it as chief executive of ITV:

One of the things that you must never do is indulge in wishful thinking. This is the time people start considering silver bullets offered by a 'transformational' deal, but silver bullets rarely exist. It is very rare that an opportunity comes along that just transforms a business. When great things happen, they happen because of really good people, good teamwork, fantastic amounts of hard work and a giant dose of luck.

I couldn't agree more with these sentiments. They fit in exactly with two basic rules to follow when weighing up a deal.

Rule number one is never to grab an opportunity simply to get you out of trouble. This might be a tactical move but it's not a strategic one, and you should always be thinking of overall strategy when considering a move. To give an example: when Asda bought Wades that was a bad tactical decision. ('We need to diversify to generate more income because we're falling behind; let's buy another business.') When Asda sold to Walmart that was a good strategic decision. ('We need to find a partner in the same sector who can help us achieve our ambition to grow.')

One of the best-known failed mergers was the $360 billion union between AOL and Time Warner, announced in January 2000. AOL was then the best-known name on the Internet (hardly anyone had heard of Google), and Time Warner controlled an empire of magazines, music, movie and television businesses. In the fanfare around the original deal both parties declared that together they would form 'the world's first fully integrated media and communications company for the Internet century'. However, the tension between 'new' and 'old' media never got ironed out and the AOL Time Warner management spectacularly failed to integrate the two companies. It was left to Google to change the world.

Rule number two is a rule I have already outlined: don't mate with what you hate. No opportunity is a good opportunity if it goes against everything you've stood for in the past. You see this with mergers and acquisitions all the time. Companies in roughly the same industry but which have been at loggerheads for years suddenly get forced into an arranged marriage. Both parties have completely different cultures, and the dominant party then tries to force its culture on the one it acquires. All too often it simply doesn't work. What's more, it brings out the petty side in people. Mergers and acquisitions often stall, not because they don't make sense, but because egos get in the way. It's the three frogs on a log conundrum: what's the new company to be called? Where's it to be based? Who's going to run it?

Sometimes, of course, such an arranged marriage is unavoidable. In September 2008, for example, Lloyds TSB sealed a £12 billion rescue deal to take over HBOS. The deal, which created a banking giant that held close to one-third of the UK's savings and mortgage market, was controversial for many reasons, not least because it had been brokered by the then prime minister Gordon Brown and because many shareholders found themselves comparatively worse off. Internally, things did not look too bright either. The team from both parties had very different feelings about their union. Helen Weir, former head of Lloyd's retail banking arm, explains:

The Halifax and Bank of Scotland colleagues felt really bruised because they had been through such a difficult time.

On the Lloyds side there was quite a bit of resentment. They wondered why we were 'rescuing' a competitor.

Dealing with this was one of Helen's principal challenges:

I picked a senior team that consisted of an equal number from both businesses, Lloyds and HBOS. I didn't do it deliberately – I did it because I chose the best people; however I was pleased that the new board was balanced. I said to them, 'I want you to check where you have come from at the door. We are a different business. A new business. Our job is to lead our business forward and a key part of that is to paint a picture of where we are headed.'

What was absolutely critical was that we had a common objective, that we as a team shared. It wasn't about the past, it was about the future. We made a clear statement – we were now 'One bank, One team'.

It was really important that, as a leadership team, we had a common vision of what we were trying to build and that we were seen to be one team leading the new business, rather than representing the old businesses from which we came. We were then able to articulate to colleagues very clearly the role that different heritages played in building the new business.

I mention the Lloyds TSB/HBOS merger to show that, as in most situations, even decisions that run against basic business principles can be made to work. In this case, the trick was to hit the ground running and pull the two businesses together really quickly. When I've been faced by any merger situations my aim has always been to complete a large part of the integration programme within the first 100 days. We always get both sides working on it together, combining people from our core business and from the acquired company and work extremely hard to make sure the balance of leadership is right. We continuously remind ourselves that we have bought this company to make it better, or because the combination with our existing businesses is better.

DECISION-MAKING LESSONS

› There are very few decisions that are
completely black and white. In many
cases, any decision is better than no
decision at all. Many people believe that
once a decision is made, it can't be
changed. However, the reality is most
decisions are flexed over time. It is
almost always possible to make
adjustments as new information
emerges, and actually colleagues
respect you more if you do. You may well
learn new things too.

› If you are simply trying to manage
tomorrow's headlines, the kind of
decisions you make will never be as
good as when you focus on the longer
term. Short-termism reduces your ability
to make tough decisions in an
intelligent way.

Helen Weir, former group executive director (retail),

Lloyds Banking Group

But opportunities that don't quite fit the usual rules need astonishingly close attention. You have to accept that there will be initial
problems, and that you must be alert to them. You also have to
accept that focus will be more important than ever – hence, for
example, the reason why having joint chairmen and chief

executives as some sort of compromise in merger and takeover situations is a disastrously weak and dangerous compromise. In other words, you have to go ahead with both eyes wide open. And you will only do that if you already know what the basic rules are: integrate quickly, fire early, get some quick wins under your belt, and stay the course.

Chapter Four

The Progress Decision

I said earlier that a large proportion of a leader's time is spent fire-fighting: either intervening to put things right or answering people's questions when they're not quite sure what to do. These sorts of decisions, however, are not what can be called progress decisions. They are certainly an essential part of everyday life, and are there to make sure that things don't go off the rails. But they don't tend to take things forward. Making a progress decision demands a different approach: here, you're not reacting to circumstances; you're anticipating and creating them.

And you can only do this if you are constantly guarding against complacency. The danger otherwise is not just that things will begin to slow down; they'll start to go wrong as well. It's a bit like riding a horse. If the horse is speeding along, it's tempting to loosen the reins and let it carry on on its own. To begin with all is fine. Then the horse slackens its pace. Then it slowly veers off course. Before you know where you are, you're late and you're lost.

You need a very particular mindset to avoid this, and this mindset is nicely characterised by Gail Rebuck – who has been at the helm of publishers Random House for two decades – as a form of paranoia. The better things are going, she says, the more you need to worry and to be wary, and this is where progress decisions come into their own.

In Gail's case, the recent rise of digital publishing – eBooks, apps, and so on – offers a good example of paranoia at its most creative. As she explains:

> The transition to digital is the major issue for publishers today. Think of it in terms of Charles Handy's sigmoid curve. Here we all are, successful publishers, at the beginning of a decline at the top of the curve. If we had not thought it through and worked hard at the emerging sigmoid curve, which is the digital technology of the future, then we would now be in big trouble. That is why we got on to it early and decided to invest massively in our digital future, even though the sales did not seem to warrant it. We also put our most senior executive in charge.
>
> In those early days digital was less than 1 per cent of turnover. Now it is growing so rapidly that we find ourselves, having made that investment, in good shape to service this emerging market. We are now running two businesses: our core business of traditional books, which is 90 per cent of what we do, and then our new emerging business which is completely different but takes up 50 per cent of our time.

DECISION-MAKING LESSONS

› You can't only make right decisions. You have to accept you will make many wrong ones. You have to build up your experience bank. All I ask of my team is that they make more right decisions than wrong and learn along the way.

› The worst kind of wrong decisions come as a result of procrastination – in other words, when you ignore the faint signals that something is not right for so long that it is allowed to become a complete car crash.

› When it does go wrong, don't play the blame game. Get on with putting it right.

Gail Rebuck, Random House Group

Gail's comments on digital publishing show three key elements of good progress decision-making: anticipation, execution and focus. Digital publishing started as a faint blur on the horizon, but the moment Gail and her senior team were aware of it, she started asking essential 'What if?' questions: What if digital publishing takes off? What if it turns out to be the future? What's the best thing it could do for the business? What's the worst that could happen if we ignore it? In other words, she set out to anticipate what might happen. Having decided that digital publishing could well take off, she then put in place a clear execution strategy for Random House – demanding, for example, that as many new and existing books as possible should be made available in a digital format, and put the whole emerging business under her deputy – to ensure it got top executive strategy and execution. But – and this is a very important point – she also maintained focus. As she says, digital publishing currently accounts for a small share of her turnover. Things may change, but at present traditional books are the key part of her business. Consequently, she kept a focus on what her company was already doing very successfully while simultaneously putting in place strategies for the future. Had she ignored digital publishing, it would have been a long-term disaster. Had she gone into it 100 per cent straight away, that would have been a short-term disaster. Her approach has been far more nuanced:

> **It is not about putting a full stop to what we do now. The tough call is not just saying, 'Right, now let's move headlong into this new market.' That is too staccato in my view. It is more of a flow, transitioning the past into the future.**

This, to my mind, is crucial and it's what characterises a good progress decision. The casual 'Perhaps we should try this' approach can result in a course of action that is at best a distraction, at worst damaging. The 'We need to consider this' approach can result in genuine progress.

This is perhaps what makes some of these progress decisions among the hardest to make. There is, after all, no burning platform. There is no urgent time imperative that says, 'Do it now, or else you'll be in a real fix.' There is simply a nagging thought at the back of your mind that something may need to be done at some point, along with another more complacent thought that you could quite easily carry on with your day-to-day business without changing anything. For now.

Val Gooding experienced this at first hand when, as chief executive of healthcare giant BUPA, she was weighing up what to do with the hospital side of the business in 2005. The group had many strings to its bow, having invested heavily in various parts of the sector over the years, both in the UK and abroad. There were, however, some question marks over the relationship between the firm's insurance business and its branded hospitals. The insurance business bought beds from the BUPA hospitals, but, to ensure ready availability in all parts of the country, used hospitals outside the group too. Equally, in order to maximise its income, the hospital business had to trade with all other health insurance companies elsewhere. In short, Val knew that the two BUPA businesses sometimes had competing objectives which were difficult to resolve.

> The question was always at the back of our minds as to whether we should sell our hospital business. It was not an easy decision to make though. We were very proud of our hospitals. They were very high performing, enhanced the brand and the business was profitable. Also patients valued the service highly. What was not to like? I also felt very proud of the employees that worked there.
>
> What eventually tipped the balance was that when we really thought about it hard, we felt the private hospital business would grow better if it wasn't owned by us and that without it we would be able to focus more effectively on our UK health insurance business.

Val did not rush into a decision, spending many months weighing up the options. BUPA's 25 acute care hospitals and one treatment centre eventually went up for sale in the spring of 2007 and were acquired by European private equity firm Cinven for

£1.44 billion in June. The timing could not have been better, in terms of the financial turmoil that was just about to hit. But, says Val, luck didn't come into it.

> I get a bit resentful when people say to me, 'You were lucky to get the sale away then.' No, it wasn't just luck! It was about consulting widely and thinking about it in depth for a long time. The market valuation of the assets was materially higher in 2007, there was a high level of interest and that meant we could do a really good deal for the hospital business, our employees and for BUPA.
>
> We had constantly kept the hospital issue on the agenda and this was the right time to act.

Paranoia is something you find again and again among the really great decision-makers. They may not call it that – they might describe it as restlessness or obsessiveness – but what all these people have in common is a constant questioning of the status quo. Richard Desmond, the straight-talking founder of Northern & Shell, which since 1974 has grown from a fledgling publishing business into a thriving media empire, is typical in this respect. He dreads complacency, even when things are going really well. He believes, as I do, that you might miss out on opportunities, or you might fail to nip a problem in the bud before it becomes a major challenge and a potential distraction. As he puts it:

> Every week I look at the magazines and newspapers which we've had for years now as if they were part of a new business. I know things change all the time and you've got to pay attention to that. If I've got a problem I sort it. I don't ever run away from it because little things become big things quite quickly.

DECISION-MAKING LESSONS

› Fly easyJet. Its fine to go on private jets now and again, but the day you lose touch with your customers and stop paying attention is when things start to go downhill. See what people are watching, what they are wearing and what they are talking about.

› Life is too short to have sleepless nights over a decision. If you don't want to do something, don't do it.

Richard Desmond, Northern & Shell

And if you think that no one is ever foolish to embark on a 'Perhaps we should try this' strategy, consider the following anecdote, told to me by Charles Dunstone, founder of Carphone Warehouse:

> I was once at quite a high-profile industry reception: lots of the great and the good in the media, plus politicians and civil servants. I started to chat to a Minister from the Department of Culture, Media and Sport and was stunned to the point of silence by what he told me. He had started off badly enough, telling me that he didn't really use the Internet and didn't really understand it either. Then he looked at me earnestly and added, 'But we need to regulate it'. That was his instinct. He didn't even know how he wanted to regulate it, or even why, but just arbitrarily decided that he needed to get control. I was totally staggered.

'My pet hate in decision-making,' Charles concludes, 'is making a decision for the sake of making a decision, so you are being "seen" to do something.'

Creating the right environment

Progress decisions are often collaborative processes. Unity is forged, not forced. Great ideas, after all, can come from anywhere. The trick is both to create a culture in which new ideas can thrive and to ensure that there is iron discipline in the way they are selected and acted upon.

I, for my part, am a great note-writer and try to send out one significant and compelling one to my top team once a month to keep things on the boil. My aim is to always give it a snappy or surprising title, so that people immediately get the gist and remember it.

Some I have sent in recent times have included titles like 'Kwik Plans', '10/4/10', 'Period of Lull', 'The Morning after the Night Before' and 'Curate's Egg'. Sometimes they're quite specific, designed to meet a particular challenge. 'Kwik Plans', for example, was an email sent out in August to counter the tendency for the summer months – when people are drifting in and out from their holidays – to become periods of inactivity. It was sent out to the top team on a Sunday night and called for five quick-fire initiatives over the five days of the working week. Monday then started with a conference call, where each person was required to brief the rest of the team on a specified aspect of his or her responsibility; by Tuesday people were expected to be able to give 30-minute presentations on what plans they had; and there were similarly tough challenges for Wednesday, Thursday and Friday.

'10/4/10' had a similar sense of urgency attached to it. The first 'ten' in the title represents ten really chunky tasks to complete and the second ten the year. Thus, there will be a ten for eleven, ten for twelve and so on as the years pass by. These memos are sent out in the autumn when there are only ten weeks to go before the end of the year. The tasks, such as rethinking a marketing campaign or redefining our format strategy are not written in such a mundane fashion though. They are written in a language or code which means something to everyone in the company but nothing to those outside. So, one might be, 'SAP 1, 2, 3 Done' which was calling for three ways to sort out our big systems. Another was 'No Frills Quadrophenia' which required four major steps forward in our 'no frills' discount format. This may mean very little to you reading this here, but, believe me, everyone in my organisation understood the code and saw it as a clarion call to action. The implication was clear. If we didn't get these things done now, how could we take the company on to the next level in the coming year?

The other two initiatives were more in the way of being mood setters. 'Period of Lull' came just after a period of constant activity when everybody on the team had been working pretty hard. It was designed to be a shot across the bows – to remind everyone that they needed to keep on their toes. Similarly, 'The Morning after the Night Before' was sent out after a particularly disastrous day in the business. I felt some bad decisions had been made and that the team needed to learn something from them, so I likened the experience to a bad hangover after an ill-judged night of excess. I wanted everyone to have a moment of reflection and to think about what they needed to do to ensure the business did not feel so bad again. And 'Curate's Egg' came in the wake of a tough quarter that, like the proverbial curate's egg, had been hard and lumpy and then soft and runny in parts. I was conveying to the team that we had only just scraped through, so had to up the ante for the next one. It was an unusual image for financial results and so made an impact. Everyone got the message.

Not all the corporate decisions that come from such initiatives will be big game changers. Many of the day-to-day ones will be more about consolidating what you have done so far and maintaining the momentum. Many will be about making barely discernable incremental improvements. Initiatives like these alter the rhythm of a company and change the all-important drumbeat. I do this often, because if you change the rhythm you can achieve a lot.

Of course, encouraging ideas will inevitably mean that people will come up with those that you don't want to act on. This needs careful handling. You have to adopt a balance between finding positive ways to turn down other people's ideas while still trying to maintain the motivation.

One way to keep ideas flowing but not too scattergun is to encourage people to find some sort of visual metaphor for the business. Every year I get my top team in a room to consider what six or seven things are really going to make a difference to this organisation. But before we kick off, I ask everyone, 'If this company was a film, what film would it be and why?' It's a useful mental exercise. It helps fix in everyone's mind what the organisation is like today. When people explain to me why they've chosen the film comparison they have, it gives everyone else a strong sense of how the company is regarded internally and externally and what it needs to do to make progress. I then ask them what film they would like it to be, and why. It's a good and very visual way to anchor in their minds what our ambitions should be, and it's also a useful reference point for future conversations.

To give a somewhat frivolous example; when I joined the Royal Mail the film I had in mind was definitely *Titanic*. My five-year movie-based vision for the business was *Rocky*, a classic triumph-over-adversity flick.

In a similar way, and again when I first started at the Royal Mail, I vividly remember meeting all 1,500 of the group's top managers in three meetings across the country. For many of them it was the first time they had ever met. Most had certainly never ever gathered in the same room in their lives. Instead of doing a major slide presentation I had two flip charts, and I asked them what they wanted to talk about. After a slightly nervous pause, because no one had ever asked them such a thing before, they all asked the question that had clearly been rankling them for years. Where had it all gone wrong? They felt irked by the negative chain of events, and the fall from grace of that once great institution, because they had done everything they had been told to do. By bringing people together in a way that was out of the usual run of things and launching the discussion from a very simple starting point ('What's gone wrong?' rather than 'How do we execute X, Y and Z policies?') I felt we had gained clarity, that the issues we had to deal with were now common to all and that we were therefore in a position to start moving forward.

I now run these sessions in most of the businesses I am involved in. 'Brief big' is an important mantra for me. Get as many people as possible to hear direct from the horse's mouth the issues as he or she sees them. If every leader could speak direct to all his or her people every day, communication would be easy. 'Brief big' is about getting as close to that as humanly possible. It's particularly important in tough times. At Loblaw, for example, we regularly got all those of VP rank and above together. One session at such meetings is called 'Your issues' when, for half an hour, we replicate the Royal Mail approach with flip charts and discussion of issues and possible answers. It's simple but powerful.

What surprises me is how few companies take the time to have these conversations about what they could be and what they could do differently. I know it's made a huge difference to all the organisations I've led – and I've heard exactly the same from other business leaders who have embarked on similar exercises. Ian Cheshire, for instance, told me that he conducted a similar exercise in Barcelona with the top 250 members of his team shortly after becoming chief executive of Kingfisher and that it generated an astonishingly strong list of ideas.

> We are a business that came together through a series of acquisitions and which always had a decentralised structure. People who worked in France in Castorama never really saw B&Q in the UK. It was only when we started putting people together that actually everyone realised that we had a lot in common. We were a £10 billion company acting like lots of different shops. Once we realised this we started thinking, could we be the best? Could we get the highest sales per square foot? The best customer rating? The best employee rating? We could start talking together about what we could do to drive this and create innovation and growth. We also spent a lot of time talking about how we could unlock all the good things that we had, without ruining all the good local stuff.
>
> The whole meeting was unconventional, held away from head office in what one wag said looked like a Russian nightclub. The

point is everyone felt able to have a series of really true conversations and came up with a massive list of ideas. It was much easier for the group executive to come away and ask, right, what is the vision, based on everything we had heard.

The worst thing you can do is to build in 'innovation' meetings to the timetable as though they're just another part of the working week. They will soon degenerate into pointless progress meetings and they're guaranteed to waste time. But if you can inject a sense of urgency into the company, along the lines I've suggested, and ensure that forums for discussing new ideas are not run of the mill or routine, then things will happen. Changing the rhythm of a company is a way of injecting a sense of new purpose and vitality into the day-to-day tasks that may be mundane but are nonetheless critical.

This doesn't mean you always have to find an unusual venue for a get-together or set aside a whole day for it. Even a humdrum meeting can be turned into an ideas meeting. The trick here is to up the ante a bit. So, for example, I always ban people from giving me lengthy presentations in meetings. Indeed, I can't stand many presentations at all. What's the point? I want a conversation, not a long list of dull statistics where you can guarantee everyone has drifted off before the second slide comes up. My opening gambit is always, 'What is happening here?' That is a challenge for the person at the other end of that question, because they're not too sure what they're going to be asked next. They know they need to be on their toes.

I well remember a meeting I held with Rico Back who came to see me shortly after I took over the Royal Mail to talk about running GLS, the Royal Mail's European parcel business. He duly arrived at my office carrying his laptop, which housed a lengthy presentation about GLS and the market it operated in.

I told him not to bother getting it out of its bag.

'Here is the job,' I said. 'You can either scale up the business, or sell it. How would you do it?'

I added that if he decided to scale it up, I would support him. If he decided to sell I would be equally accommodating. Rico has since told me that the experience was extremely unsettling, as he had spent many days honing his presentation and he felt rather as though he had been thrown into the deep end of a very cold pool. However, that didn't come across at all. My memory of the meeting is that the two of us had a long, honest and very constructive conversation about GLS. We got a huge amount done, agreed a strong strategy and set in train a series of events that have made GLS the successful business it is today – the fastest-growing parcel business in the world and the real 'Kohinoor' of the Royal Mail. If we had gone through the presentation he had planned to show it would have taken at least three or four further meetings to get to that stage and to be honest, the luxury of time was not something we then had at any of the Royal Mail businesses.

Picking winners

The really great decisions are often the simple ones, the ones where after the event people say, 'I can't believe no one has thought of saying that before.' They're a bit like suitcases with wheels. Both the wheel and the suitcase had been around for ages, but it took a long time before someone came to the obvious conclusion that the two might work well together.

Not every decision, however, has to be a truly great one on some sort of epic scale. Smaller-scale good decisions are also valuable because they will bring about incremental improvements. What's more, by encouraging an environment where good decision-making flourishes, you make it possible for ideas to come along that will truly transform things.

An example of what might seem in strategic terms a relatively straightforward decision, but to my mind a good one, came in my early days at the Royal Mail. At that stage I was regularly chatting with the posties and they happened to mention that not long before I joined, the powers-that-be at head office had changed their standard issue shoes, jackets and pouches in which they carried the letters. Apparently, the new shoes were cripplingly painful and both the jackets and pouches let in the rain. So what did the helpful souls at head office do when the postmen complained? They disciplined anyone found not wearing the regulation shoes and jackets, or not carrying the pouches.

Making a decision to fix this may seem like basic common sense, as indeed it was: after all, the last thing you want is posties with sore feet and soaking mail. But it was important for other reasons, too. It signalled a change in management style. It showed the posties that people were listening to them and doing something about their concerns. It dealt with an immediate problem and also fed into broader decisions about company culture and attitudes.

Even on a larger scale, it's extraordinary how often the solution to an apparently intractable problem turns out to be a very simple one. A classic example of this came in my early days at Asda, when we were pushing through an exhausting programme of store renovations in 1993. We had embarked on an ambitious strategy of renewing 40 stores in the first year, at a cost of £2.5 million a store.

We thought they looked great when they were done. There was just one problem: sales at the revamped stores were going through the floor. I couldn't understand why this was happening. Surely, attractive, revamped stores should be more appealing than clapped-out old ones. What on earth could have gone wrong?

I went to talk to the store managers to find out if they could shed any light on the problem. They came up with the answer straight away. 'Well,' they said, 'everything is in the wrong place. There is no flow to the store, the customers can't find anything, and they say it's difficult to shop.'

I walked around a newly refurbished store and could see in an instant they were right. The frozen food was in completely the wrong place and products that are traditionally adjacent to each other were scattered halfway across the shop. No wonder people were not spending any money. In fact, I was surprised more of our customers had not simply abandoned their trolleys and walked out in frustration.

In the rush to sort out the ageing stores, we had fallen into the classic trap of putting aesthetics ahead of the actual use of the design. We had become a builder, not a retailer. On paper, the problem we faced seemed bizarre and paradoxical: improvement was apparently leading to a decline in sales. Once we had actually isolated what the problem was, the solution was simple and practical: put things in the right place and people will buy them. It really was as easy as that.

As for an example of clear thinking that led to a breathtakingly audacious decision, I can think of no better than a meeting at BSkyB I attended shortly after I joined the board in 1999. I'll never forget it. There we were, listening to some fairly gloomy news. BSkyB was seeking to become the dominant force in digital television, but it was facing stiff competition and wasn't making much headway. Indeed we were facing a heavy financial loss.

Some good ideas were coming to the fore, and we had just got the Premier League Football contract. Then Rupert Murdoch looked up at the group of worried people around the boardroom table and said, 'Firstly we need distribution. Then we build content. Then we deliver the best production technology in the world. That's our model. And we start by giving away the set-top boxes for free.'

Responding to looks of surprise he added, 'We need distribution. If we don't have distribution, we are not going anywhere.'

And so the decision was made.

Many people looking at this decision in purely commercial terms might have baulked at the move. After all, BSkyB was having a tough time and, having had two years of modest profits, was looking at making a substantial loss. To compound the problem by offering set-top boxes that retailed for £200 for nothing seemed, at the very least, counter-intuitive.

But as soon as Rupert made the suggestion, we all knew he was right. My background in retail told me that distribution is essential. The worst that could happen if we went ahead with Rupert's plans is that we would lose more money, but then we were haemorrhaging cash anyway. The best that could happen would be that the enticement of a free set-top box would bring us millions of subscribers virtually overnight. It wasn't just the right thing to do. It was the only thing to do.

It also arose from asking a very straightforward question – How do we get more subscribers? – and coming up with a straightforward answer – offer people an irresistible deal. It's an approach that works time and time again. So often people will come at a problem from an oblique angle, asking subsidiary questions rather than the one that matters. It would have been so easy for Rupert to have asked for example, 'How do we improve our broadcasting?' or 'Should we show more sport?' – neither of them bad questions in themselves, and certainly the sort that many intelligent people would ask. However, by coming up with a question that went straight to the central problem – lack of customers – he was able to make a decision that was both brilliantly simple and very audacious. I choose the word 'audacious' advisedly. This was not some panicky, risky, bet-the-company-type decision. It arose from known facts and was entirely in line with what BSkyB wanted to achieve: to be the major player in the new digital age.

Feargal Quinn, who made his name as founder of the Superquinn grocery chain in Ireland, offers a similar story about the Irish postal service An Post, of which he was chairman back in 1984. Things were pretty grim when he took over. Previously, An Post had been part of a broader organisation that also ran Ireland's telecommunications, but now it was on its own and suffering badly. It was losing money, morale was at rock bottom and the organisation had just suffered a 19-week strike. To make matters worse, business was booming for the telecommunications business, now a separate concern. Feargal recalls:

> I knew that the telecoms guys were about to launch a four-minute ad on TV, crowing about how they were fixing the phones, plus loads of banner ads in the press too. I thought, What can I do? Once my team see this, they will be even more upset at being forced to move across to the old-fashioned, ugly sister.

Feargal found it easy to articulate the questions that needed to be asked. How do we improve morale? How do we find more business? Now he needed to find the answers. And they came in the course of a dinner conversation.

I decided 'to hell with it' and invited six of the best marketing people in Ireland to dinner on the basis that sometimes you don't have to pay for advice if you offer people a nice meal. I said to them, 'How would you suggest we start? We can't afford ads like the telecoms people. We can't afford to pay more to our staff.'

One of them, a man called Jerry Liston, said, 'Would you ever think of reintroducing the Penny Post for a short while?' The Penny Post had come to Ireland in 1840. Jerry said, 'Everybody would talk about it and it might encourage people to get around to writing letters again.'

As a result, I sent out to all of the 2,000 post offices a load of one penny stamps and went on the *Late Late TV Show* to announce that, the next day, anyone who posted a handwritten letter (I wanted to avoid the banks and the tax man sending their bills out on the cheap) could do it for a penny. Many people hadn't written a letter for years and the number of letters that were posted the following day was huge. The postmen were very busy, the post offices were very busy and suddenly everyone was talking about how marvellous the An Post was. Plus, one in four people who got a letter replied four days later. So, we got a huge boost at full price. My own local postman couldn't get over it. Suddenly everyone was pleased and excited about being involved. Everything after that was a lot easier.

DECISION-MAKING LESSONS
› It is good to trust others to help you with your decisions, but you need to do your own homework too to understand whether the advice you are getting is well founded.
› I've always looked for consensus, rather than have a vote. However, there are times when you have to hear it all and just say, 'This is the way we are going to go.'
› Never compromise on the essential aspects of your business.

Feargal Quinn, Superquinn

All this can seem like a moment of unique inspiration. And it is. But you can see that by breaking the problems down to their simplest component parts, answers do suggest themselves. What's more, such intuitive leaps can occur anywhere. Dame Julia Cleverdon told me of a great example at Business in the Community (BITC):

> Back in 1991 there was a riot in Oxford where cars were broken into or stolen. There were all sorts of newspaper headlines about Dreaming Spires and Burning Tyres. It turned out that a lot of lads were pinching cars around the Blackbird Leys Estate and driving about.
>
> I rang John Neill who is chief executive of Unipart, which was a big Oxfordshire business. I said, 'Can you help Business in the

Community understand what is happening?' He sent two young engineers down to speak to the kids to discover what had happened and why they were pinching the cars. The boys were quite clearly obsessed with cars and said in a cocky fashion they could get into any car in the street. 'Show us,' said the engineers, and sure enough, click, click, click they opened everything.

One of the engineers went back to John and said, 'We need some way to engage these kids, to show them that if they stay in school and do what they are told they will get a reward.' The reward that Unipart came up with was that if the boys behaved themselves, they could go and work on Unipart cars, mending them, putting them together and racing them. They started a project called Trax which unlocked the talent of those young people and helped reduce crime substantially.

Meanwhile, having seen what they had done, the other engineer went back and invented a car immobiliser device which has itself reduced car crime dramatically.

Such innovative thinking should always be there if you encourage your team and create the right environment for them to brainstorm. It doesn't matter if some of their ideas are wild and wacky. It's your job to filter those out. The point is that people in the team are relaxed enough to throw ideas around and know they are not going to get laughed at. Sometimes, this may even mean that you have to step out of your comfort zone and consider an entirely different angle. You may have to be a bit more flexible than you would normally like to be. That is great, though. No company ever got great by staying the same.

DECISION-MAKING LESSONS

› Once you succeed in getting one thing done, there is always a domino effect where others are then more willing to join in.
› Do your homework. If you want people to come with you and support you, find out more about them, especially their early influences.
› The real leaders are the ones that can get everyone energised behind a decision in a way that makes it fun and challenging.

Julia Cleverdon, Business in the

Community

Gail Rebuck at Random House actively encourages innovative thought in her line of business. She freely admits, however, that sometimes when considering new projects she has to open her mind to something so entirely new that it can seriously challenge her preconceptions. One such project turned into an unlikely best-seller:

There has been a trend for celebrity autobiographies for a while. Some years we have more than our fair share of number-one best-sellers and other years the same books just don't work. It has a lot to do with how good the books are, of course, but also how authentic they are, how well written and how much they match public taste at the right moment.

The managing director of one of our divisions called me and

said she wanted to talk to me about making a reasonably high offer for a book.

'It is the autobiography of the meerkat from the television adverts,' she said.

My first reaction was, 'I am sorry, I can't believe you are suggesting this to me.'

She said I really needed to see the publisher and hear his pitch. So I agreed. The publisher came in and did this amazing presentation that totally convinced me that this had been properly thought out. He saw a significant humour market for this book. It was his passion and authenticity, and the extent to which he already had a good and interesting track record at slightly off-centre humour projects, that convinced me. He sees things that others don't see, which is precisely what you want in an editor. We went ahead and *A Simples Life* became one of our biggest best-sellers in 2010, selling over half a million copies.

Keeping the impetus

One of the biggest challenges with progress decisions is to keep them coming. When you make a good radical decision or a decision in a crisis that may well be good enough – you're looking at a specific challenge or problem and if you've found a way to tackle it – then it's job done. But progress decisions are not like that. They're the life-blood of any company, and if they're not constantly pumping them into the system then the company will die. The problem, of course, is that people always have a tendency to slow down if they feel that they've just done a great job or pulled off a bit of a coup.

Justin King has faced precisely this challenge at Sainsbury's. Back in 2004 he and his team launched the 'Making Sainsbury's great again' recovery programme. The plan was a simple one: to revitalise the then ailing store group by focusing on good-quality food, excellent customer services and retail basics such as keeping shelves fully stocked. It's succeeded brilliantly and Sainsbury's is now getting the thumbs-up from shoppers and the City is complementary about its steady growth. In 2010, for example, profits increased 9 per cent. However, Justin has been at pains to keep things going even after a run of good results. As he explains:

> Making Sainsbury great again was a powerful idea because it never felt like it was a destination that we would reach any time soon. Of course we are a lot better than we were, but great just moved. While we have been busy getting better, our competition has too. Greatness is not a moment in time; greatness is a journey, which has a long way to travel.
>
> In 2007, I was asked in an interview whether I thought we had made Sainsbury's great again. I said, 'No we haven't. We've achieved what we said we would do but I still worry about three things: consistency, complacency and capability.'
>
> I know I can walk into some of our shops now and they are fantastic, the best there are in the marketplace. However, for every great one I walk into, I can still walk into one that isn't and we won't be a truly great company until all 900 stores are fantastic, consistently, week after week. There is never any room for complacency.

There is a balance to be achieved here, though. There's a big difference between keeping up the push for continued excellence and appearing to move the goalposts ever further back. The former approach is essential; the latter can be very demotivating: you can't keep the team slogging away, year after year, with no acknowledgement that they have done a great job. At Sainsbury's, therefore, Justin was careful to mark the supermarket's success at a key moment when it moved from recovery to growth:

A really important part of big, difficult decisions is making sure you complete the story with something that says, 'Isn't this fantastic; we achieved X'. There was a day when I sent out a note to all our colleagues saying, 'You remember that two and a half years ago we said we would grow to £2.5 billion of sales? Well we're pleased to tell you that last week we did. Tomorrow, to celebrate, we are going to give all our colleagues a 20 per cent discount.'

It's worth noting, though, what was going on behind the scenes:

By the time that note went out, the £2.5 billion was no longer what we were thinking about, because we were already on the next stage.

Part 2

Road-testing a Tough Call

Chapter Five
Testing the Vision

Decision-making is not a science. However brilliant you may be you're never going to get every call right. It's quite possible, for example, that you make entirely the right decision but that circumstances then conspire against it.

Surinder Arora experienced this at first hand with his hotel group when he decided to build the £272 million, 605-bedroom, Sofitel London at Heathrow Terminal 5 and to buy a property portfolio from BAA for £315 million.

Both decisions made complete sense. The gleaming glass and steel Sofitel is the largest luxury airport hotel and convention centre in Europe, attached to one of the busiest airports in the world – a great hotel in a great location. The property portfolio purchased from BAA helped consolidate Surinder's position in a key area of the hotel market which lies at the heart of his business.

There was just one problem. Timing. The glitzy, celebrity-strewn opening of the Sofitel took place in July 2008, just weeks before the collapse of Lehman Brothers. The BAA property deal went through a month later. Suddenly companies started pulling in their horns and cancelling foreign business trips. To make matters worse Terminal 5, which had opened in the spring of that year, was still suffering a wave of negative publicity as it sought to cope with teething problems: numerous flights were cancelled due to 'staff familiarisation issues', check-ins were temporarily suspended and tales of missing and lost luggage were rife. It was not a great season for a hotel launch.

As Surinder recalls:

> It was all a bit of a challenge. The T5 property didn't deliver anything like what we thought it would deliver in the first seven months and as for that property portfolio, well, I guess in that first three months I lost about £120 million. It was the right deal but wrong time.

Even more depressing in some ways is the right decision made for the wrong organisation. Dame Julia Cleverdon recalls a particularly galling experience at Business in the Community back in 1997 when she was looking for ways to counter the high reoffending rate of ex-prisoners. The initiative began with a visit to Reading jail with David Varney, who at the time was chief executive of British Gas.

> David asked the prison governor his percentage rate of return and the man said it was about 80 per cent. David said, 'By God, if I was managing to retain 80 per cent of British Gas customers I would think we are doing really well, but as I am paying for your failure, that is an absolutely appalling statistic.'

It soon became apparent what the problem was:

> The governor explained his belief that they didn't return if they
> had a job. David decided to test that thesis and asked him to pick
> 50 of the most likely lads. British Gas would then train them to
> be forklift truck drivers because the firm was always short of
> them.

It was a bold gamble but the results of the experiment proved to
be beyond Julia's wildest dreams. Six months later, only 6 per cent
of those on the scheme had reoffended – and magnificently
National Grid Transco developed the programme to take it to scale
with their suppliers.

But that was the good news. Persuading the public sector was
more difficult:

> David became completely incensed about why the prison service
> would not help roll out the programme. He and I trailed every
> single government department that might be in charge of the
> prison service to say, 'We've done this. We know that we could
> get a lot of these characters straight by giving them jobs.'
>
> After months of discussions, compromises and brick walls,
> we got nowhere. I remember standing on top of the Home Office
> steps with David. He turned to me and said, 'The problem with
> talking to the prison service is they are like goldfish – they know
> nothing other than the water in which they swim. They are not
> prepared to do it in a different way.'

In both Julia's and Surinder's case, things didn't turn out as
planned, but that doesn't make their decisions wrong. As Julia says

– patience and never giving up is the greatest virtue for a campaigner. And while the initiative Julia describes hit the buffers, Surinder's business enterprise eventually came good. Fortunately, although he had stretched himself, he hadn't over-extended the business:

> I comforted myself that, as a group, we were strong enough; otherwise I would have been cleaning tables again. I decided that what we all needed to do was work smarter and harder. We did and within months we turned around the hotels and now we have done better than our expectations with the property portfolio we bought, too. We now have nine new hotel projects coming through over the next three years on the back of it, some of which we are building for ourselves and some which we are selling on. We are in a much better place than we started in now and the experience has made us much stronger.

DECISION-MAKING LESSONS
› You can always make mistakes. It is only strong people who make new ones. Sometimes you have to be brave.
› Gut instinct is important and you need to be able to trust everyone around you. In any relationship, whether it is work or home, if you don't have that trust you will never be comfortable in your decisions.

Surinder Arora, Arora Hotels

Surinder's decision was based on a sound premise. His hotel empire was built on the airport business. It therefore made sense to do what he did – arguably the BAA property portfolio was just too good an opportunity to miss. It may not have been a perfectly timed decision but at its core it was a good strategic one. Similarly the situation Julia describes may not have led to a decision that was fully executed, but that doesn't detract from the strength of the strategy.

Compare these two problematic decisions with the one made at Boots in 2000. Already a highly successful pharmacist and retailer, it opted to diversify into becoming a health care provider as well. Suddenly chiropodists, laser hair removal parlours and dentistry services sprang into being on the upper floors of all its stores. There was just one problem with this plan: it didn't work. Boots might have been a brilliant retailer, but it simply didn't know anything about the service side of health care. What's more, it failed to realise that it was offering services that none of its customers associated with it. After four years, the health care experiment was scrapped.

This was the wrong decision at the wrong time, in the wrong place, for the wrong business. It never stood a chance. To that extent it is reminiscent of one of the biggest corporate mistakes of modern times: the launch in April 1985 of Coca-Cola's New Coke. Designed to meet the challenge posed by Pepsi, it was hopelessly ill-considered. Introducing New Coke as a new product line might have worked. But by deciding simultaneously to abandon manufacture of a drink that generations of Americans had been brought up with, Coca-Cola didn't just deviate from what had made them great, they threatened to destroy it. It came as no great surprise to most people when, seventy-seven days later, 'Classic' Coca-Cola was reintroduced.

Of course, it's easy to point out errors in hindsight. At the time, people would have made perfectly cogent arguments for taking Boots into health care or moving Coca-Cola on to a new product. To that extent, two very bad decisions could be said to be have been as logically made as, say, Surinder's or Julia's, which both seem to me to have been good ones. And that poses a major question. When you're mentally road-testing a decision how do you tell the difference between possibles and no-hopers?

Know what you stand for

I am a great advocate of simplicity. If you cut to the chase and isolate what it is your organisation is meant to do, what it does well and what it wants to achieve, then great, focused decisions will follow. Always ask yourself what your company is. Answering this question in one sentence is a discipline that will keep you on track and the business focused on what it is – and will also act as a filter to stop programmes that are about what the business isn't.

So you have to start by ignoring the over-complex and the irrelevant. That may seem obvious, but it's extraordinary how difficult many organisations find that to do. The entire banking crisis of 2007 and 2008, after all, essentially came about because bankers so overcomplicated their own business that even they didn't understand it. Helen Weir was only too aware of this when she joined Lloyds Banking Group in 2004 as financial director. Prior to this she had held the same role at DIY giant Kingfisher.

Banking is an inherently complex sector, but bankers can complicate it for England! Lots of clever people seem to want to make it as convoluted as they can.

Her view was that everything needed to be simplified:

In my former life at B&Q we bought stuff and we sold stuff. At Lloyds, we bought stuff and sold stuff too. It is just that what we bought and sold happened to be money, but that is effectively what we were doing.

One of the things that first struck me in banking was the focus on products, as opposed to customers. My take was, let's start with the customers. It doesn't matter how good a product is – it is only worth having if it meets a customer's needs.

It is about changing how an organisation thinks. Just like any retailer, banks have to understand their customers' needs and how they can fulfil them.

Many firms have learned this to their cost. Even Apple, one of the globe's best-known brands, had a serious stumble when it forgot what it stood for in the early 1990s. In a knee-jerk response to intense competition from PC manufacturers, the firm introduced a profusion of new Macintosh computers, including the Quadra, Centris and Performa. There were too many models with very little variation in their technical specifications. Even the most ardent Mac fans were confused. Somehow, Apple had forgotten the essence that had established its reputation: simplicity. It took the electronics giant years to recover from this mistake and it only really found its way when founder Steve Jobs returned in 1997.

Sometimes over-complication leads to situations where people actually forget what they were supposed to be doing in the first place. This is particularly the case in companies in crisis or facing particular challenges. Adam Crozier, who has worked on turnarounds at the Football Association, Royal Mail and now ITV, notes that when things are not going well the temptation is to introduce targets and goals that are both hard to understand and a distraction from the basics:

> It is a great trick, but it is quite easy to spot, even from the outside. I often read in the papers about how one company or other judges how well they are doing and think, What on earth is that measurement all about?
>
> I've experienced it first-hand many times too. When I went to the Football Association they couldn't wait to tell me how many friendlies they won against the big teams abroad. I said, 'It doesn't matter. It only matters when you play them in a competition. A friendly is a friendly; that is the whole point.'

Perhaps Adam's most extreme experience of this came at the Royal Mail:

> I remember going into a big mail centre and asking how was it going.
>
> 'Fantastic,' they said. 'We have an EP ratio of 80.'
>
> I said, 'Is that good?'
>
> 'Yes,' they said. 'Last year we were 77.'
>
> 'Great,' I said. 'Out of interest, what is EP?'
>
> They had absolutely no idea. EP, or earnings price ratio, is a mathematical formula to measure a firm's expected earnings over the coming period, but it was complete gobbledegook to

them. Apparently though, it made everyone feel absolutely tick-etyboo about how it was all going.

Adam then went on to find a not dissimilar situation at ITV:

> If you look back into its history, they would often talk about how their market share had remained relatively constant. What they were actually doing was constantly redefining the market. So, it began as share of television, then it became share of terrestrial television and then moved on to share of commercial terrestrial television.

DECISION-MAKING LESSONS

› Decisions about people are always the toughest. You should take it very personally and worry about getting them right. If you don't feel like that, you should get out.
› It is OK to compromise, but the decisions you generally regret usually involve some sort of compromise that you were never really comfortable with.
› There is no point trying to move on and create a new direction, until everyone has stopped being defensive and accepted what the problems were. You must be united around a new strategy.

Adam Crozier, ITV

What all this means is that before you embark on making decisions you need a clear framework for them, and you do that by having a very clear vision. Archie Norman, who has had experience of no fewer than five turnaround situations at Woolworths, Asda, Energis, Coles and ITV, puts it very succinctly:

> When you are leading an organisation, particularly one that has not got a track record of success, people want the religion. They want to know, 'What are the principles? Where are we going? What are we trying to achieve?'

It's extraordinary how difficult many companies find it to articulate their vision. Most mission statements are hopeless. They are so vague and so full of anonymous corporate speak that you could quite easily delete the name of Company A and insert Company B. They express fuzzy claims ('We are focused on delivery' – who isn't?) and even fuzzier aspirations ('Our goal is to become the market leader through excellence' – again, who isn't?).

Mission is straightforward. Ask yourself, 'What will this company be when it grows up?' *Purpose* is, 'Who are we satisfying?' *Values* are 'What are the ways we want to do things around here?'

Strategy is simple, too. Think journey, think compass. The strategy is: we are heading north. *Tactics* involve deciding which roads to take to get there. Inevitably, tactics or execution change sometimes. If the road is the M1 and you know it's blocked further on, do you just sit there, or do you find another route?

To illustrate what I mean, I'd like to look in a little detail at two strategies that I have been involved with: at Asda and at Royal Mail.

At Asda we decided very early on that the expression of what the supermarket was to be – its compass direction, if you like –

was eight words: Britain's best value fresh foods and clothing superstore.

Every word had significance. We wanted to be seen to be British, because all our competitors were going abroad and we were staying as we were. We wanted to be seen as best value, because that's what Asda was traditionally known for. We wanted to be seen as purveyors of fresh food, because it's fundamental to a supermarket's success and was something that Asda was hopeless at. We wanted to be recognised as a clothing retailer because we could see that this would be a good part of the market to be in and, with the George brand, could help differentiate us from the competition. And we wanted to be a superstore, because that is more ambitious than being a supermarket.

What we had in those eight words was a restatement of our core values and an expression of our goals and aspirations. We wanted to go back to being recognised for offering good value, because that is what had made Asda successful in the first place. And, having done that, we wanted to build.

So what did we do?

To begin with, we never missed an opportunity to display our Britishness. So, for example, when other supermarkets were pulling British beef off the shelves at the height of the BSE crisis in 1996, we took the opposite stance and banned all foreign beef.

When it came to fresh food, we went back to basics. We stopped hiding all our produce away at the back of the store and brought it right to the front. We reduced the ranges to concentrate on getting those we did have right. We improved our supplier base and began building up the skills amongst our colleagues. We were the first supermarket to introduce apprentice schemes in our bakery and many of our colleagues went on to do City and Guilds qualifications.

When it came to value for money, we never stopped telling the story of 'Asda price' because we knew we had to re-establish our credentials as the best-value grocer. 'Asda price' was not something the business just invented. It came from genuine conversations customers used to have when they went around our stores. They used to point out goods and say, 'That's an Asda price.' Of course, at that time they were more likely to be pointing them out and saying, 'That is not an Asda price.' It was 'Asda price' that lay at the centre of our strategy and we built all the other values of the business around that. As it turned out, 'Asda price' proved to be the barometer of our success. When we stuck with it we did brilliantly; on the rare occasions we strayed from it, we didn't.

At Royal Mail, our mission was to become the world's best postal service. Everything followed from that statement of intent.

First of all, I knew that if we were to offer a first-class service once again we had to simplify and economise. That's why we scrapped the second daily postal delivery in February 2002. When I examined it, I realised it was a myth: delivery was actually pretty patchy and many people only got a second post once a week. It was also a massively expensive myth: the second post represented 4 per cent of the total volume of all mail delivered but absorbed 20 per cent of our delivery costs. Getting rid of the second post saved a fortune and allowed us to focus on improvements where they would actually count.

I've made that sound simple, and it was certainly a logical thing to do. But it was also a classic tough call. The commercial case was obvious. The customer case was too, in reality, since most people didn't receive a second post. However, the emotional case was far harder and what one could describe as a media 'gimme'. And it was a political issue, too. Leadership, however, is not a popularity contest, so the commercial imperative had to outweigh other considerations.

And if you think that all companies aim at simplicity, consider the time that I discovered 15,000 brand new bicycles and 15,000 pairs of size seven boots in a warehouse in Swindon. You might charitably think that this was because someone had decided to rationalise the postal service by only employing posties with size seven feet. In fact, it was because some bright spark, realising that they were ending the financial year with a slight surplus on their budget, decided to buy a job lot. The fact is that most companies overcomplicate. The better-run ones do it because that's what humans tend to do. The badly run ones do it because complexity is a great way to deflect people from the truth.

Incidentally, the drive for simplicity doesn't just involve things you should do. It's also about the 'Not to do' list. In fact, a very good discipline for any head of a company is to compile a 'Not to do' list twice a year. Initiative and programme creep occur in all organisations and hamper execution of the main tasks. They become clutter. Formally decluttering and culling ideas that are distracting or low-priority helps liberate what is essential.

In the same way, another useful injunction is to 'Bayonet the wounded'. Every organisation has projects that limp along because they happen to have a sponsor or trigger some sort of emotional attachment – some small subsidiary, for example, that has always been around but has never actually worked. Such entities are not just worthless, they are distractions and hold the group as a whole back. You have to isolate them, and then bayonet them.

The sort of detailed strategic plans I've just outlined depend, of course, on getting that fundamental compass direction right. If it's wrong, you have to rebuild from scratch and, as I said earlier, that's often a difficult thing for a company to achieve from the inside. As Adam Crozier says:

> In many cases, when you see a company that so clearly needs to change but doesn't, it is down to the fact that the top team don't actually believe that the company needs to change and therefore, funnily enough, they don't.
>
> Brutal honesty about where you are and how you are performing is crucial. A company can't move on unless people are aware of the issue. Not only what the problems are, but also, if they do this or that, where are they going to end up.

When the fundamental compass direction is right, however, then the big decisions start to slot in. Take Tesco, for example. Back in the 1990s Tesco, along with other supermarkets, recognised that the food business was becoming increasingly saturated and mature. Growth would have to come from elsewhere. Now there are lots of ways that could have been attempted, from organic growth to acquisition, and there are lots of ways in which costly mistakes could be made. Remember Boots: it might superficially have seemed logical to extend from pharmaceutical goods to health care, but it forced the chain to move into areas that it didn't understand and that its customers failed to connect with. By contrast, Tesco knew that its first priority was to keep its low price pledge. Everything flowed from that. The strategy Tesco chose was to build up its non-food offering with goods such as CDs, DVDs, books, clothes and homewares.

Tesco's already huge size allowed it to be more efficient in its buying process than other high-street specialists. From the moment it tackled the area, its non-food range was on sale for the best price around. Tesco also ensured it did not fall into the Boots trap, by bringing in high-street specialists on everything from fashion to technology. Finally, on top of being able to offer the keenest prices around, the supermarket made the most of its innate advantage – convenience. Shoppers were already coming into the store regularly to buy food, so, by placing the non-food right at the front of the store in large displays at great prices, they could hardly lose.

And you can see the same thing happening today with the major grocer's move into banking. A potentially risky strategy, it's understandably been embarked on in a cautious way, with just a few products such as insurance and credit cards on offer. But where it's working it's because it ties in closely with the fundamental values of the company concerned: good value, good customer service and convenience.

This focus also pays dividends when a decision needs to be made fast. If you already have a strong sense of basic direction, then even massively complicated and fraught negotiations can be brought to a swift and satisfactory conclusion.

This was certainly true for BBC director general Mark Thompson when he embarked on what has been described as the toughest licence fee negotiation for a generation. The months in the run-up to the decision in late 2010 were rife with claim and counterclaim about what might or might not be at stake. The culture secretary Jeremy Hunt started the game of hardball by declaring at the Edinburgh International Television Festival in August that, 'the BBC has to live on the same planet as everyone else'. There was talk of shifting the cost for free TV licences for the over 75s from general taxation to the BBC, and making the corporation responsible for funding the World Service. In the end, it all came down to a few hours of frantic negotiations to produce a deal that left the licence fee flat at £145.50 and the BBC facing making savings of at least £300 million over the next few years. It was as good as, or better than, any settlement the BBC could have expected in the economic climate that prevailed.

As Mark recalls:

> We had done a lot of work on the BBC's budget and had detailed business plans and economic modelling for the next Licence Fee period. The BBC's governing body, the BBC Trust, was behind us. It was our idea to go for the settlement we did. I said to the secretary of state, Jeremy Hunt, 'If you want us to take on the funding of the World Service and all the other stuff, we could potentially, but only if we can agree a multi-year settlement.' Jeremy said, 'Is it really possible to agree a Licence Fee deal in a week.' I said, 'Why not?'
>
> I had absolute clarity over the parameters of a possible deal. I knew what would be acceptable and what would be unacceptable. I knew the zone of outcomes and where we needed to get to so we could continue to deliver the highest quality service to the public. It is critical to have a clear agenda in a high stakes process where you know you are going to reach a decision about something rapidly. Yes, there are high personal and professional consequences when you are engaged in a tight pressurised negotiation. But through that whole period it is fair to say I was in a fairly decisive mood.

No plan survives first contact . . .

One of the toughest lessons to learn in business is that not everything you do is going to turn out perfectly. As I've already said, you're doing well if you get your decisions right 70 per cent of the time, and if you wait until you're 100 per cent certain then the chances are that you will never achieve anything at all. Progress and momentum is what you're aiming for. Not perfection.

That means that even when you've mentally tested a decision and it feels absolutely right, you have to accept that you may need to modify it in the light of developments. Modify, not change. Move too far from the basic premise of the decision and you have to start again. That doesn't mean, however, that you can't accept some trade-offs and compromises along the way. Good leaders follow the 70/30 rule in most areas of their professional lives. In this case, the rule means accepting trade-offs about 30 per cent of the time, and knowing that if they come away with 70 per cent of what they wanted they've done very well.

Used creatively, compromise or trade-offs can be quite a motivating tool to get people to see a new way around problems. I often challenge my team by setting them tough targets and initially make it clear that I am not prepared to take anything less. Thus, for example, if I know it takes 26 weeks to build a new store, I will tell them I want it done in 11 weeks. 'Go and find a way I can have a new store built in 11, or we won't be building any more.' If they then come back and say to me, 'Allan, we can't do the store in 11, but we can do it in 13,' I will say, 'Good.' Have I compromised? Yes. On the other hand, I have just got a new store built in half the time the team originally predicted and can see that they are getting better and better.

Setting ambitious, stretching goals is a tactic adopted by Martha

Lane Fox, the government's digital champion. Charged with finding new ways to help disadvantaged people use new technology, the founder of lastminute.com decided in 2009 that the brief she had been given did not go far enough. She therefore issued a challenge to get the entire country online by the opening of the Olympics in 2012. This is clearly no small undertaking: when she threw down the gauntlet 17 per cent of the entire population had never been online and many felt excluded by their economic or social circumstances.

It was a risky decision on many levels. There was a risk that it wouldn't happen; there was a risk that the whole project would lose momentum; and it was personally risky for my own reputation.

The alternative, though, was that we just chugged along and did stuff around the edges.

DECISION MAKING LESSONS
› Cut through as much irrelevant material as you can, to simplify a problem before making the decision.
› If a decision goes wrong, take the time to have a debrief among the team to discuss it. It can be very helpful and will generate positive feedback.
› Things will go wrong. Be prepared for it, learn from it and move on.

Martha Lane Fox, UK digital champion

By setting such a challenging goal, Martha may have stuck her neck out, but, in practical terms, she was also able to galvanise big corporate partners such as the BBC, Google and TalkTalk into action. After all, they wanted to be part of something that felt important, ambitious and good for the country and now someone was setting a very concrete challenge. Whatever ultimately happens, Martha's initiative will prove far more productive than one that is 'safe' and unambitious:

Even if we don't get everyone online by the Olympics, we have the partnership structure and campaign which will get us there and will continue beyond. I have no doubt that we have gotten to where we have done a lot more quickly by working this way. It is always best to be as bold as you can be.

It's also important to acknowledge that when any operating plan is first devised, not every last detail of it will have been thought through. Part of the plan therefore has to be to allow for some details to be planned later. I usually have half a dozen things on my 'plan to have a plan' list at any point and always make sure these come up for discussion at the next big strategy or planning meeting. Of course, it could be that, as we continue down the line, we realise that a particular detail needs more or less attention or indeed no attention at all. Either way, we are still keeping our sense of direction.

As General Lord Richard Dannatt would attest, the old adage that no plan ever survives first contact with the enemy is certainly true, and it applies to business just as much as it applies to warfare:

There is no problem with plans changing, providing you understand that it might happen. In the army we talk about 'question

four'. This refers to the fourth question that we always ask when we are analysing the missions we are given, which is, 'Has the situation changed since my superior gave me my orders?' If the answer is 'yes', then you go right round the analysis decision loop again. Rather than be worried about it, you need to go back and examine the factors you examined before when you took the original decision.

You only do it if you sense the circumstances have changed. Otherwise you have done your analysis, you have made your decision and you get on with delivery.

We always tried hard not to compromise too much at the Royal Mail. Our feeling was that people had done that far too much over the years and that is why the business was in such a state. Compromise, of course, has to be in the mindset but it should never be the mindset. And you can never compromise on anything that imperils the Holy Trinity of good business: mission, purpose and values.

Ultimately, you need to keep your eyes on the prize. It's always very interesting to talk to people who are not quite at the level of chief executive yet, but who are clearly heading in that direction. If you ask them what aspect of the top job has the greatest impact on them, they will invariably say, 'Direction' or 'Lack of direction'. There is nothing worse than being given no direction, with the person at the top being persuaded in this way or that and seemingly changing their mind with the wind. What you want is for a leader to listen, weigh up and say, 'This is what we are going to do. It is up to you guys to decide how to achieve it, but this is what we are going to do.' That's direction.

In extreme situations all bets are off, of course. There's no point pressing on with something when circumstances are stacked against it. Take the recent developments in News Corp's lengthy negotiation to buy the 61 per cent of BSkyB it does not already own. The move has been mired in controversy since it was first announced in June 2010, with rival media companies insisting it will reduce media plurality to an unacceptably low level. Along the way, Business Secretary Vince Cable, who had been tasked with deciding whether to approve the bid, was stripped of the responsibility after making unguarded remarks to undercover journalists that he 'had declared war on Mr Murdoch'.

In March 2011, Culture Secretary Jeremy Hunt announced that he was minded to accept undertakings that News Corp had offered to get approval for the deal – subject to public consultation. However, commentators said that News Corp had been forced to make greater concessions than it wanted to by agreeing to spin off Sky News into an independent public company. How did James Murdoch feel about this at the time?

Compromise decisions are never easy, but you can break them down. There are a handful of things to consider when you are assessing the conditions to do one thing or another. You have to keep in mind the terrain you are on, the prevailing environment, the people you are dealing with and their motivations and what you are trying to accomplish. Then you have to consider your own ability to see things through.

Above all, you have to remember what the goal is. To a large extent, that means being able to get and maintain a sense of perspective. If you are aware of a range of considerations and aware of how they interact, my sense is that getting to a decision is more straightforward. Once you have perspective, you

understand where it is you are trying to get to and there could be a variety of ways to get there.

In early July 2011, however, another part of the News Corp empire, the Sunday paper *News of the World* became engulfed in allegations about phone hacking. As the crisis escalated, News Corp announced that it was withdrawing its bid for BSkyB.

Chapter Six
Leadership v. Consensus

You've got a tough call on the starting blocks. It may be a major one to help stave off a crisis or a minor one to improve a particular aspect of your company. On whatever scale it is, it feels right to you: it's easily comprehensible, it deals with a real issue and it's completely in line with overall strategy.

And then you start discussing it with people . . .

The objections can come in many forms. It's a terrible idea. It's a great idea, but is this the way to do it? It's a great idea, but is this the time to do it? It's a great idea, but who's going to carry it out?

This can be pretty disheartening but it's also inevitable. Very few ideas that really make a difference go through on the nod. If they do, the chances are that they won't make much of a difference and that's why no one has objected. As Sir Martin Sorrell says of his own company WPP, which employs 140,000 people:

The biggest threat to WPP is not the competition, it comes from within. The enemy is people not working together, lack of response, slowness, tardiness, arrogance and complacency.

Before you assess the validity of an objection, it's as well to know why it's being made, and it's often possible to work this out from the overall nature of the company.

Generally speaking, companies in crisis or with a particular problem are those least likely to give an idea an open-minded hearing. The chances are that their view of the world is skewed: they're in denial about what is going on; even if some individuals are aware that there are difficulties, they won't see them as their fault or responsibility.

This was certainly Ian Cheshire's experience at Kingfisher. At one time, he says, squabbles between the various subsidiaries in the UK and abroad resembled those between medieval barons:

> **At that stage we had two divisions, one in the UK and one in France and they endlessly fought each other. There were also tensions between the stores and the e-commerce operation too. B&Q people were openly hostile or scathing about those in the Screwfix online business. Brico Depot and Castorama virtually refused to acknowledge each other, even though both were in the French DIY business. It was like the old feudal baronies.**

Even within relatively happy companies, there will be tensions, as different departments or individuals assess how a particular decision will affect them. Take the retail environment, for example. If you are thinking of making a decision that is going to have a cost implication, everyone will have a differing view. If they're at the centre, they'll want to spread the cost at store level. If they're at store level, they'll want the cost off their balance sheet and either charged back to the centre or taken by the supply chain. Everyone may well be behind the decision in principle, and they may accept intellectually that it's in line with the company's strategy to offer the consumer the best possible price, but they still don't want to be the ones to lose out.

The difference between the two scenarios is that in an unsuccessful company the chances are that the basis of the decision will be challenged; in a successful company the basis will probably be accepted but the proposed execution may be challenged. This calls for some clear thinking on the part of the leader.

The three stages of decision-making

Every well-executed decision has three parts to it. There's the strategic: 'What is this decision aiming to achieve?' This is where the big ideas are initiated and the analysis is done. There's the operational: 'How do we put this decision into action?' This is the planning level, if you like, where the big idea is translated into a credible plan. And there's the tactical or execution level, where it all happens: 'Now, let's make it happen.'

All three elements should be up for discussion in a well-run company – otherwise what's the point of having intelligent people around? However, before embarking on a discussion, you should always bear in mind Lord Dannatt's golden rule:

While tasks can be delegated, responsibility never can.

This is a key consideration, and spreads right down the decision-making process from strategy to execution. Any decision-maker has to accept that while they may choose to take on other people's ideas or entrust others with the task of putting a plan into an operation, they can never pass on responsibility at the same time.

Lord Dannatt gives a telling and chilling example of the ramifications of personal responsibility, recalling the time he gave evidence for the prosecution at the trial of Radislav Krstic before the International Criminal Tribunal for the Former Yugoslavia at The Hague. General Krstic had commanded the Drina Corps of the Bosnian Serb Army at the time of the capture of Srebrenica and the subsequent massacre in Eastern Bosnia in July 1995.

> **General Krstic's mistake was to accept a mission from his superior General Ratko Mladic, which directly led to the massacre of 8,000 Muslim men and boys. He had accepted ownership of the mission and therefore became responsible for the plan. Had he not accepted it, or talked General Mladic out of the plan, then he would not be in prison now and those people would still be alive.**

Lord Dannatt clarifies the lessons to be drawn from this:

> **This issue of ownership and delegation is very important. Of course you delegate tasks, but you never delegate responsibility. It is what we call mission command. A leader looks at what has got to be done and then frames their intent with a capital I.**
>
> **Describe to your people what it is you need to achieve, then delegate the tasks and supervise appropriately what is going on. The buck, however, always stops with the boss.**

DECISION-MAKING LESSONS

› Take expert advice, but always trust your own judgement. Trust and respect your own leadership ability. Recognise that you have made a decision and people have to go with what you have said.

› You can't be everywhere at once to make sure these things happen. A good leader should get to the centre of where the main effort is occurring, putting themselves in the place where they can have the most influence.

› Compromise is often thought to be a weakness. But if compromise is more of a balance of conflicting interests and might bring on side more stakeholders and opinion formers, then it shouldn't be seen as a weakness, it should be seen as a strength.

General Lord Richard Dannatt

Anyone who takes this rule on board will approach decision-making in a very particular way. They will know that they can't shirk responsibility if they allow someone else to make a decision that then goes wrong. They also know that they are responsible for the decision-making process every step of the way. It's not enough to come up with a good strategy and then fumble the execution – and while you can certainly criticise those who are delegated to carry out the plan if it goes wrong, you can't comfort yourself with the thought that the mistakes made are solely their responsibility.

When to listen, who to listen to

Bearing this in mind, you need to know how far you are prepared to listen to others and take on board what they say. The way I approach this is to establish in my own mind before any meeting how much I'm prepared to move on a decision – whether it's with my team or external people – and at what point I will draw a line in the sand. That provides me with the mental boundaries I need. Obviously, I'm prepared to be flexible on certain issues. As I've said before, if a leader is utterly dogmatic and refuses to be swayed by the arguments of others, what is the point of having them there in the first place? And if your starting point is, effectively, that you don't trust your team to come up with sensible opinions, then you have a problem that goes way beyond how best to make a particular decision. However, if you have set out to surround yourself with the best people you can find, taking on board what they have to say is the logical thing to do. It's also good for the organisation: it sends a signal that everyone in the team is valuable. A bit of give and take goes a long way.

In fact, it is quite rare for anyone on the team of a well-run company who disagrees with something to disagree with it fundamentally. Usually, they disagree with something on the basis of the impact it is going to have on them, or they don't think that a particular action is right at that time. If you take the time to listen to them, and I mean really listen, it is quite likely that you will see that they have a point. It is up to the person at the top to make a decision on whether to change that particular aspect, or move on. If you have listened well, that choice is usually quite easy.

But there's a caveat here. Bearing in mind Lord Dannatt's point about personal responsibility, I always guard against seeking consensus for its own sake. In any negotiation the person responsible for making decisions has to understand that if they compromise too far they actually change the essence of what the decision is about. If that happens you can't allow things to meander on. You have to start again. You have to find a different solution.

In my own case, I certainly want a good range of opinions. I also expect lively discussion and generally expect that at the end of it we'll all be on the same page. But if necessary I'll call the shots. Once that's happened everyone is expected to buy into the decision. This is collective responsibility. It's not consensus. Consensus, in my view, is overrated. Asda's Andy Clarke summarises this attitude well:

> If a leader becomes completely belligerent and never changes his or her view then they lose the confidence of the people who work for them. However, total compromise is a weak place to be.
>
> If there is a big decision to be made and I strongly believe that it was the right thing to do even when everyone else thought it was the wrong choice, I would always take the leadership role. I would always say, 'I am going with what I want to do.' If I didn't and went with everyone else, what would happen when it all went pear-shaped? I'd be left defending a decision I hadn't agreed with in the first place.
>
> You can't duck behind other people for the really tough decisions. When the buck stops it always stops with the chief executive.

The Royal Mail's Moya Greene sees things similarly, arguing that in her organisation she constantly has to balance a strong personal sense of what needs to be done with a willingness to listen:

> We are at a point in this company where things are in pretty stark relief and there are not 100 options. There are two or three. But, when you are dealing with 155,000 people, two very powerful, very knowledgeable unions, a bunch of regulators and more government departments with an interest in this than you can shake a stick at, it doesn't pay you to be too dogmatic. That said, because I need so many things to come together to save this company, I am also going to be pretty clear about what is needed and when it is needed.

So when you're making a decision, who do you listen to? In a successful company, you will have a strong team on whom you know you can rely. That doesn't mean, however, that they will all sing from the same hymn sheet. Just because everyone appears to understand a decision and is apparently full square behind it, doesn't mean to say that they don't have their own very firm views about it. Mix that in with the inevitable human struggle for power and status, rivalry between departments and the odd personality clash and there is the potential that the tensions could spill over to conduct that could seriously spoil the smooth execution of a decision.

I happen to think that tensions can be creative, challenging people to analyse their thinking more carefully. The old 70/30 rule usually applies here. Within a typical team, even allowing for some turf wars and personal animosities, you'll get good views and agreement 70 per cent of the time. The other 30 per cent of the time internal politics finds its way in, and you need to watch out for that.

› Devote at least 25 per cent of your time to communicating your decisions to everyone. Make sure your managers do that too.
› Always have the difficult conversations. If you don't, the problem won't just go away.

Moya Greene, Royal Mail

This sort of input can come from any level too. There was a classic example of this during my time at Asda. I was on one of my frequent store visits when I got talking to a lady colleague in our bakery section. 'Do you know why there are so few female bakers in the company?' she asked. 'It is because the hours are so ridiculously unsocial that there is no way working mums can fit in with them.' She was right. Our bakery team started their day at 6 am to make sure the bread was ready for 8 am. No employee with children to see off to school could possibly work around that sort of schedule.

My colleague went on to point out that many women like baking, that they're good at it, and that Asda was missing out on a pool of talent by being so dogmatic about working hours. And as I listened to her, I realised she was absolutely right. The practice of early baking was actually a throwback to the days of the traditional high-street bakery when bakers used to get in at the crack of dawn knowing that people would buy bread and cakes on their way to work. This no longer happened – in fact the peak bread-buying hours are between 11 am and 4 pm these days – yet no one had thought to change an old tradition that made no sense any more.

I decided we had to do something about this. If we redesigned the daily schedules, we'd get more able people involved and we'd be offering our customers really fresh produce at the time when they wanted to buy it. It seemed so breathtakingly simple, and it came about not because the person at the top said 'We must do this', but because the person at the top listened to someone in the team saying 'Why don't we do this?'

In the same way, a challenge from people you respect can also prove invaluable. When I was at the Royal Mail, as part of the programme of cost-cutting, the decision was made to put an end to all employee awards. The awards, which had been in place for many years, recognised length of service and were for ten years, 15 years, 20 years and even a quarter of a century. My original thinking was that they were a luxury we couldn't afford. My senior team, though, didn't agree. They pointed out that at a time when we were pushing through so many tough changes, we needed to reward loyalty and good service. I realised they were right, and I changed my mind. In fact, we then decided to make the awards an even bigger deal, adding an annual Chairman's Award to celebrate achievements in the workplace and in the local communities the posties served. It made a visible difference to morale at the Royal Mail. The team had been completely right to question the original decision.

There's also a lot to be said for making a quick mental calculation as to the scale of the impact a decision is likely to make, and then deciding who in the team can make it. If it's a major one, then the person at the top should make it. If it's not, then the appropriate person in the team can make it, with, of course, everyone else buying in, including the leader. Dalton Philips, chief executive of Morrisons, has, in my view, got the balance absolutely right:

There are calls that you have to make, big calls on integrity issues, or you might go down to the wire on a budget and disagree when people want to put this number in or that. Alternatively, you might have to make a decision on some big marketing campaigns, but generally if the decisions are grounded on data, the whole process is a lot easier to do. Why not include your team?

Occasionally you may have to overrule, but you can't be this central decision-making machine. I have a team of senior people who I know can make good decisions. If I have to make decisions for them, I don't need them.

Some leaders do all that because the macho thing still goes on. The use of 'I' in the boardroom is a long way from dead. In my view, it is much better to be selective when you make a decision.

These big positions are about empowering your team, getting them to go the extra mile and do extraordinary things. If the person at the top makes all the decisions they will never do that.

Sometimes, though, you need a completely fresh and disinterested view, and this is often the time when it's good to call on outside advice. I'm a strong believer in using consultants on occasion. However, you should never ask them to do something you're not prepared to do yourself or think that by calling on their services you can somehow put off a difficult decision.

It's often the case that executives have a tendency to call in the consultants to act as some sort of shield between them and an unpopular decision – for example, the business of laying people off. They feel that by being once removed from the process, they can somehow show that they are the nice guys and all the nastiness is down to someone else. It's not going to work.

That said, the right consultant can be fantastically useful. I don't believe in calling on endless armies of them, but I am totally committed to having a relationship with one or two key people. A good example is Michael Mire at Mckinsey. Over the years he has become part of the furniture at every company I have worked with. Although he knows and understands the way I think, I find it refreshing that he will almost certainly bring a different perspective to bear on a particular issue. It is a bit like having a top notch insider, with fantastic insight into a company, but with the ability to use outside resources to support their thinking. He works closely with the internal team – crucial both to keep everyone feeling involved and because the consultants bring a rigour to thought processes that should rub off on and inspire the rest of the group. Working with them is a bit like drilling for oil. Together we put in a lot of boreholes. Not all will prove productive, but sometimes you hit oil.

I don't want to imply here that if you ask enough people they'll come up with a decision for you. They can help you frame your questions and challenge your own assumptions, but to leave everything to them would be to delegate responsibility. And as I've already said, that's not an option.

The fact is that on occasion you will have to make decisions that fly in the face of received wisdom and everything people are telling you. Martin McCourt at Dyson has first-hand experience of this. Back in 2002, the company was wondering whether to tackle the American market. It wasn't an idle thought that came from nowhere. They already had some experience of the North American market, because in the early days of the company James Dyson had struck a licensing arrangement with Fantom, a company based in Canada, for the US market. He had done this in the hopes of creating a constant revenue stream, but over time the company had come to dislike the arrangement:

> Fantom marketed the vacuum cleaners as a specialist, premium-end product, whereas we wanted them in as many mainstream stores as possible so every American would have the chance to buy a Dyson. Then, as we were storming away in the UK, across Europe, New Zealand, Australia and Japan, something interesting happened. Our competitors saw what we were up to and started to imitate us by coming up with their own bagless vacuum cleaners which were also brightly coloured with clear bins. The major manufacturers in America used their distribution muscle to push their bagless vacuum cleaners and Fantom got squeezed. They panicked, cut corners on costs in manufacturing, the quality went down and they were in Chapter 11 before they knew it.
>
> We immediately sent our top guys to Toronto and bought the rights back from the receivers. I am still amazed our competitors stood by and let us do that, but that is another story.

Dyson now faced a stark choice: carry on or pull out. They asked a lot of people for their opinion. Most advised the company to pull out. After all the US market is notoriously difficult and is littered with the corpses of failed British ventures. To try and then to fail would involve a big financial loss.

Inevitably, one or two people suggested a compromise approach:

> We consulted with a lot of very experienced people who knew America better than we did and they said we should take a biopsy

approach. We were advised to take some of the Eastern seaboard, maybe some of the independents and wholesalers too and see how it goes.

Martin wasn't convinced. Sometimes it's easy to convince yourself that what in reality is a half-hearted approach is a sensible gently-gently one. He decided to go for it all out:

I devised a strategy, which was called 'Go as far as we can, as fast as we can'. The idea was to massively gear up and capitalise to target all the major retailers in America.

This was a high-risk strategy. As Martin himself says, 'Yes, we did bet the farm a bit, but we decided to trust our instincts.' But for Dyson at this point in their evolution it was clearly a risk worth taking and although the final decision may have seemed a gamble it was arrived at through a very considered process – note that Martin talked to a lot of people, even if he didn't ultimately decide to take their advice. As it happened, his gut instincts – and his decision – were vindicated. Dyson now has a 35 per cent share of the American market.

Of course, there are some occasions when there really is not room for lengthy discussion, movement or compromise. This is often the case when there's a crisis and very few viable options. There may well be an old guard resisting the inevitable, but the way forward tends to be clear to those who want to see.

One of the hardest rapid-fire crisis decisions a leader will have to take is when the business is not performing after a period of relative calm. A business quarter is only a matter of weeks and sometimes you may not discover until close to the end that you are not going to hit your target or expectations. But, as soon as it becomes obvious that you are underperforming or heading for a profit warning, or are running out of cash, decisions have to be made pretty quickly. There will be the pressure of getting the news out to the markets, while at the same time announcing a credible solution. If things are really serious and, let's say, one area of the business is underperforming badly and it's become a pattern, you may need to make a personnel change and you need to do it fast. On such an occasion, you want people to back you but may simply not have sufficient time on your side to listen to all the arguments and take account of them.

This sort of situation is becoming more and more the norm. And what makes it particularly tough is that you have to have one eye on what's happening internally and one eye on how things are being received externally. Investors appear to have three criteria for judging a company's performance: consistency of performance (with an emphasis on both words), lack of volatility in the share price, and, finally, sentiment. You tend to find that when things go wrong, all three of these become black marks against you. Then you have a serious problem.

In tough times, markets – and investors – are more volatile than ever. What's more, everything happens in a media spotlight where bad news sells newspapers. At such times a fine balancing act is required. You want internal unity while those outside may well be baying for blood and suggesting that someone or other needs to go. If you think you've got the right team in place you have to have the courage to stick by them and make it clear to the critics that what is going on is a blip, not a trend, and that the foundations of the business are still secure. These days, blips can be twelve months, not twelve weeks. On the other hand, if there is a weakness in the team, you have to move. One of the toughest calls in the current economic environment is when to deliver a head and when to resist.

And, of course, one factor that overrides virtually all other considerations is that no decision-maker can ever appear to be indecisive. Yes, you need to ask others for their views. Yes, you can modify your own views in the light of what you hear. But if you start prevaricating you undermine company confidence. And even if you don't feel you can give a decision straight away, you need to make it clear that one is on its way. As Archie Norman says:

> Early on, of course, you may not exactly know what the answer is and may want to hold back until the next stage before revealing your big decisive moment. That's OK. 'Maybe' is not a bad answer to give people as long as they know that decisions are going to be made, how they are going to be made and what criteria will be used.
>
> I've worked with indecisive leaders and know that it can be infuriating to everyone around them. These people cannot make a choice without painstakingly weighing up all the data and evidence available and also creating an alternative plan B in case the first decision goes wrong. Most of the time they will get the decision spot on, but by then they will have driven everyone to distraction. Meanwhile everyone will have gone off in different directions trying to second-guess the eventual decision.

DECISION-MAKING LESSONS

› Most of the biggest decisions are not
  tough. You build up to them over a
  period of time, you know they will
  happen and when the moment comes
  you know what to do.
› One of the things to watch is leaders who
  have a single bat in decision-making.
  They may be effective dealmakers, or
  sales makers, or negotiators, but they are
  not going to be enduring managers.
› If you exude direction and confidence
  from the start, you will buy enough time
  and space to make the real decisions.

Archie Norman, ITV

Seeing it through

Bad decision-makers think it's all about the big idea. Come up with
the strategy, they say, and leave it to others to work out how to
execute it. General Lord Richard Dannatt's early experiences in the
army led him to see things rather differently:

> My first tricky leadership challenge was on my second tour of
> Northern Ireland. The piece of Belfast I was responsible for was
> slap bang in the middle of the sectarian divide and there was an

issue over housing. As a Second Lieutenant, I was delighted when I heard that the General Officer Commanding Northern Ireland was due to visit my patch. I explained the problems as I saw them. 'So, General, what should I do?' I asked.

He put his arm on my shoulder and replied; 'Richard, we've got broad shoulders in the British Army, just muddle through!'

To me, though, there is always a better way. You can't just leave it to the imagination and initiative of the folk on the ground. You have to plan.

When it comes to making a plan happen, always remember: 'Execution is not an act, it is a habit.' When companies get things right from time to time, it is simply an act. However, when they get them right most of the time, it is a habit. That's what an organisation that wants to be great needs to aim for and it's what great organisations have in common.

Some organisations are brilliant at execution. The BBC is a classic example. Although it has the reputation for being an unwieldy and high bureaucratic organisation, the habit of getting things done, on time, as planned, is actually hard-wired into its DNA. It is a habit which director general Mark Thompson learned during his earlier role as editor of the nightly BBC One news bulletin, formerly broadcast at 9 o'clock:

The 9 o'clock news always went on at 9 o'clock. There is a moment when the second hand gets to 12 and the programme goes on the air. If you were the editor of that programme, you would have had to have decided what the headlines were, what the top story was and how you were going to handle it. Everything would have to be organised so the reporters were there, the newsreader had

the right words and so on, right the way through the programme, every day.

In a way the whole of the BBC is like that, whether it is David Attenborough and *Frozen Planet*, or the Proms. We are very good at operational stuff because things have to be there on time, as billed.

Achieving this involves a whole range of operational decisions that are just as important to get right as the big picture. And since it's at the operational end that most people in an organisation work and therefore the most opinions – often widely diverging – are likely to be found, it's also at the operational end where discussion of and agreement on the action to be taken is absolutely crucial.

A very effective way to ensure this happens effectively is to stage a 'Big Board' day for the senior team four times a year. Big Board days are quite literally days focused on big boards. Huge, three-by-three-metre whiteboards, to be exact. The process kicks off with six of these massive boards being placed side by side in a large meeting room, charting the actions of the operating plan in giant letters. Generally, there need to be around 50 actions for the year. Each action point will have the name of the person charged with executing it written beside it, and the date by which it should be achieved.

The night before the Big Board meeting, everyone in the senior team is invited to pay a visit to the boards. Those with their names on any of the large displays must put a tick with a green pen next to the points they have successfully executed, or a cross with a red pen on the parts they have not yet been able to complete. It's a simple yes or no.

The following day, with the entire senior team gathered in front of the big boards, each individual named on those displays is invited to stand up and explain where they are on any given action point, whether it has been missed, and, if so, what they are doing about putting that right.

My rule of thumb, as usual, is the 70/30 rule. A good score is 70 per cent green ticks – in fact 70 per cent is the best I have ever seen. It is not a huge problem if everything is not perfect. You'd need to be nervous at 50 per cent, but even that is not an insurmountable problem. If, however, I am faced with a ratio of only 20 per cent green ticks to a sea of 80 per cent red crosses, this to me is a clear indicator that there is a major problem. This may be with execution; it could even be to do with the basic plan. Whatever it is, the problem is now out in the open and can be dealt with.

The best thing about the Big Board days, apart from the obvious peer pressure to get things done and not be seen to be the one lagging behind, is they give everyone a 360-degree perspective of where the company is versus its plan. Everyone can see what must be done and fully understand the need for it. Without this, people get tied in knots, worrying about their own part of the plan, with little thought as to how it affects things further down the line. Now they can see not just their part in the plan, but the context in which it fits into the whole plan. It is a very visual tool. Plus, while someone is standing up in front of perhaps 200 colleagues to explain which bit they have not done, it is the perfect opportunity to ask for some help from other departments.

What about the naysayers?

Discussion is good. Disagreement is inevitable. But what do you do if time and time again you come up against individuals who resist every decision? Such people can be immensely disruptive – they're the sort of 'internal terrorists' mentioned earlier, and ultimately they have to be dealt with.

The first step is a shot across the bows. Ian Cheshire at Kingfisher has first-hand experience of this. Faced with endless bickering between the French and British parts of the company, he felt compelled to step in:

> I was lucky that the Kingfisher management conference came five days after my appointment as chief executive so I was able to stand up and address the senior management team straight away. I told them that we were going to run the company very differently and that not everyone would make the journey. I added that it was up to them to make the choice as to whether to come along, but I thought it was a great opportunity. There was a notable frisson around the room from people who had, until now, clearly thought I was that nice chap who didn't say very much.

That warning note – that not everyone would make the journey – was probably enough to bring the occasional troublemakers back on side. For the more hardcore disruptive element, though, a very clear future direction was set out:

> I said, 'Right, one person will run the UK, one person will run France, and another will oversee our other international oper-

ations. There will also be a new financial director and the five of us will collectively run the business.'

The inevitable first reaction, according to Ian, was disbelief. 'People said, "What do you mean?"' he recalls. 'We can't do that. Screwfix wants to compete with B&Q, Brico Depot hates Castorama and it will never work.' However when it was clear that that was exactly what Ian meant the mood shifted: there was 'a stunned silence as people realised things were indeed changing'. A few people still had to go, but for most it was a wake-up call.

Ultimately, though, persistent naysayers have to go, and it's perhaps interesting to look at this process briefly through the eyes of a naysayer rather than a decision-maker. Sir Stuart Rose, who believes as strongly as I do in the importance of collective responsibility in decision-making, told me of a situation when he was the person who had to walk. It happened early in his career when he was at the Burton Group and found himself in profound disagreement with a major decision made by his then boss John Hoerner:

I did not agree with the breaking up of the Burton Group in 1997 to turn it into Debenhams and Arcadia. I faced up to John Hoerner over the weekend and we had a huge row. What happened next? He won because he was chief executive and the board backed him. I was in a minority situation. I could swallow it to keep my job, or say, 'I am off.' I said, 'I am off.' That was my choice. I didn't agree with the decision so violently that I couldn't just sit there and swallow.

There's no bitterness here, though – simply an acceptance of how things work:

> Business is democratic to a certain extent, but it is still a commercial enterprise and the chief executive is paid to make the big decisions. Those below him or her can either stick with the decision under the terms of cabinet responsibility, or if they can't they should take the ultimate sanction.
>
> It is that expression that the Americans use: 'Shut up or ship out.' If you don't like it, off you go.

I hasten to add that I don't think this is about being seen to be tough for its own sake. Decision-makers are not there to smash others into a pulp; they're there to get the best possible outcome for their company. They are, if you like, benevolent dictators, not despotic tyrants. They listen; they modify their approach if necessary in the light of what they hear; they decide. At the same time, while they encourage discussion and disagreement, they cannot afford to live with dissent. Dissent stunts progress.

Chapter Seven
When to Change Your Mind

It was Mars' 'Coke moment'. There we were with one of the most successful and iconic chocolate bars around, and suddenly sales seemed to be plummeting. There was no problem in the market as a whole. We weren't, for example, in the depths of some recession so profound that people could no longer afford treats. Nor had we upped the price of a Mars Bar. Nor had we changed the packaging. So what had we done wrong?

The answer, it turned out, was that we had fractionally altered the actual nature of a Mars Bar, reducing very slightly the 'bite height' – or thickness – of the chocolate that covers the caramel layer. There were sound financial reasons for doing this: chocolate is the most expensive ingredient in a Mars Bar, so a substantial amount of money could be saved by cutting its use back a bit. However, in making this slight and financially worthwhile adjustment we had forgotten the customer. The bite height might sound a technical nicety, but it's what gives the bar its distinctive texture and flavour. Consumers noticed straight away that something had changed, and now they were voting with their wallets.

It doesn't take a genius to work out what Mars should have done in these circumstances – and it's exactly what we did. We restored the bite height immediately and sales recovered. Soon we were back where we had been before.

Put like this, changing a poor decision very quickly sounds the easiest thing in the world. You make the initial decision. Empirical evidence shows that it's not working. You work out why it's not working. You change the decision accordingly.

But that's not how most people operate. Decision-making involves thought and emotion. A good decision-maker will think through an idea before they execute it and seek to anticipate major problems. In so doing, they put a lot of themselves into that decision. It becomes *their* decision. So if it happens to go wrong, not only do they have to make a major mental adjustment ('Perhaps this carefully thought through decision was wrong . . .'), but they have to hold up their hand to it as well ('. . . and I accept it was something I said we should do').

Taking the emotion out of decision-making is therefore essential, and a lesson we all have to learn. Some find out sooner than others; Ian Livingstone, now chief executive of BT, is one of those fortunate enough to be in the former camp. His recollections of time he spent early on in his career at the high street electrical giant Dixons serves as a useful lesson in the power of cool objectivity. Shortly after he joined in 1991, he recalls, he was despatched to the US to sort out Dixons' troublesome outlets there. The group had acquired Silo, America's third largest power retailer in 1987, and had gradually built up the number of outlets across the States, but it was hard going and the enterprise was haemorrhaging cash.

After working 16 hour days, seven days a week, for nearly two years trying to fix things, Ian had inevitably grown a very close emotional attachment to the US division. His efforts were clearly bearing fruit, too: the subsidiary was making a profit for the first time and sales were steadily growing.

However, when it came to deciding what to do next, he forced himself to be very self-critical and as objective as possible:

> I went to the board and made the recommendation to sell it, which I think surprised a few people. My reasoning was that if we put in another big input of cash we could actually make it into an acceptable business, but on a risk reward basis we would still be better off investing in expanding the UK business. It was a tough decision, but I had to take the bigger view of the long-term prospects of the group.
>
> There is always a temptation to stick with something because you have become committed to it and have invested emotional capital. But if you realise you are not being as objective as you might normally be, you have to be harder on yourself in your decision-making process.

Dixons' share price rose 20 per cent on the announcement in 1993 that the group was to sell most of its stake in the American shops to US retailer Fretter Inc. Ian's decision was further vindicated by the group's strong performance in the UK in the years that followed. In fact, Dixons became one of the best-performing FTSE stocks, launching such powerful UK players as PC World and Freeserve.

DECISION-MAKING LESSONS

› Don't become a prisoner of your past decisions. If you see that something is not right, change it.
› It is useful to take the contrary view to other people's decisions – it forces them to justify and understand why they make that choice.

Ian Livingstone, BT

As I've already been at pains to point out, you can't get decisions right the whole time. Sometimes you'll get it plain wrong, as we did at Mars. Sometimes your decision will be a good one, but the timing of it will be against you. Surinder Arora's opening of the Sofitel hotel in Heathrow's Terminal 5 at the height of the financial crisis of 2008 is an example of this. Sometimes your decision will be a good one undermined by circumstances beyond your control, something that happened to the Wal-Mart founder, the great Sam Walton, who painstakingly built up his first store in Newport, Arkansas, only to have to start again from scratch elsewhere when the landlord decided to switch the lease to his son. Sometimes you may even have to make a really tough call when the evidence for it isn't fully there. As former M&S chairman and chief executive Sir Stuart Rose says:

> You can't rush into a decision, but the worst crime you can commit is knowing you have got to make a decision and not making it. Procrastination is not an option. You have got to do something.
>
> Even a wrong decision is in some circumstances better than

no decision at all. People would rather be led by someone saying, 'I don't know if this is going to take us anywhere, but I am going to make a decision, and that is we are going to go left.' They would rather do that than all stand around and say, 'Which way are we going to go?'

In other words, there is a whole raft of reasons why you're not going to get it spot on every time. I would say again that if you are getting your decisions right 70 per cent of the time you're actually doing pretty well. And as important as getting that 70 per cent right is to recognise that, by the laws of maths, that means you're likely to get 30 per cent of your decisions wrong. This calls for a delicate balancing act between huge initial confidence and forensic subsequent examination. Justin King summarises this very nicely:

Part of being chief executive is to be almost insanely confident and committed. At the same time you have to have half an ear open to the fact that you might be completely wrong. You need to keep listening. I believe this is where a lot of businesspeople go wrong. They don't maintain that second bit. They are so convinced that they have to keep going and be seen to be confident, committed and unwavering about every single decision, that failure becomes an inevitable consequence because they stop listening.

Of course, there is a very fine dividing line to this. It has the potential to be completely self-fulfilling if people always think that big decisions are still open to negotiation, as opposed to it having been made and all the energy and effort now has to be about making the best of that decision possible, not on picking it apart.

You just need to keep your ears and eyes open, so you never

plough on regardless, long beyond the point that it became clear that it was the wrong thing to do.

So when you're hit by the repercussions of one of your inevitable 30 per cent wrong decisions you need to react. And the first step along the way is to have an attitude that will set you along the path of putting things right.

The right mindset

Even accepting that there is a problem is something that more stubborn-minded decision-makers find hard to do. If you look at companies in crisis, it's generally the case that it's the people inside the organisation who are least prepared to acknowledge the problems that to outsiders seem very obvious. Part of the issue here may be white noise – there's so much going wrong that people don't know where to start. But pride and sentiment come into it, too, and there really is no room for either in a good decision-maker.

Here is British curry magnate Lord Gulam Noon on the dangers of sentiment:

> Sentiment has no place in hard business decisions. If people go on sentiments, they will lose out. I was extremely keen to start a travel agency business about 20 years ago and opened one in India. It lost a lot of money quite quickly, so I told my partner, 'Kill it.' To start it was a big decision, but to kill it was an even bigger decision. I decided to try again in the UK, but again it failed. By then I had spent a lot of money, but it was clear that it

was never going to work. So, I said, 'Bury it.' There was no market for my idea. I decided not to try it again. I am now very happy in the food business. If the worst comes to the worst and nobody buys it, I'll eat it.

As for pride, it's an understandable human reaction, but it's at the very least unhelpful when things are going wrong. Great business leaders make mistakes and they're big enough not to let personal pride get in the way. Superquinn founder Feargal Quinn, for example, who has also had an extraordinarily successful career as a politician in his native Ireland and as a lecturer on business, is the first to admit that one enterprise he embarked on was a mistake. Back in 1999 he set up Tusa, a small banking operation to complement his supermarket group. It was a co-venture with TSB, and based on a similar in-store banking operation in the United States. It had a lot going for it, from very competitive mortgages to car loans, and it initially grew quickly into a 14-branch network employing 75 people. But then things stalled. As Feargal recalls:

With hindsight, I think the biggest problem is that we decided to put bankers in to run the place, rather than our own customer-focused people. I have always been passionate about customers and customer service, but thought I didn't know enough about banking so I had better get outsiders in to set it up and run it, instead of promoting from within as I usually did. As I later discovered, the bank in the American supermarkets had done so well because it was run by retailers and complemented the main grocery business.

DECISION-MAKING LESSONS

› Tough decisions are not always necessarily for the betterment of the business. Sometimes you have to take a view, take the hit and walk away.
› Experience is very important, no matter how important and powerful you are. There is no short cut to experience.
› Loyalty goes both ways. It is not just a word. Weigh all decisions according to the situation and the circumstances. Ask yourself how many people will get hurt and how many people will benefit.

Lord Gulam Noon, Noon Products

Quite simply, Tusa failed to convince a sufficient number of customers to desert traditional banks. Feargal acknowledged the mistake and then moved quickly to close things down.

> I was very sad about closing Tusa. I realised very quickly that it wouldn't work but really regretted having to let all the people go. Many of them had come to Tusa from good jobs in banking elsewhere because they had confidence in me and the company. It wasn't their fault it didn't work. I had to act fast and got them all together one evening to tell them the news myself.

Tusa closed in November 2001.

What people often tend to forget is not just that there's no shame in making a mistake – after all, we all make them – but that there's no shame in admitting to one, either. Leaders are often terrified that accepting something has gone wrong is an admission of weakness and failure. Actually, in my view, taking it on the chin is a sign of strength, and people who say 'Yes, I got it wrong' on occasion grow rather than diminish in stature.

General Sir Mike Jackson regards this ability to take responsibility for a poor decision as a crucial feature of a good military leader. Apart from anything else, it's essential to preserving that bond of trust that should exist between those who lead and those who are led. The example he gives is one that every young officer experiences – the moment in a training exercise when he gets his men spectacularly lost:

> We all get lost. It'll be 4 o'clock in the morning, pissing with rain and everything is as black as hell and suddenly you realise you have no clue where you are. It happened to me as a young officer and it is embarrassing. You just have to say, 'Sorry guys, I screwed up.' They'll probably reply, 'All right, boss. Don't do it again.'
>
> However, the young officer who bullshits and says he knows where he is and is just taking a clever route will have the boys rolling their eyes and thinking, 'What a load of crap.' That mutual respect will be eroded because the boys know that this young officer is lying.
>
> Trust is very important in teamwork. In the military, it is absolutely bedrock vital to have mutual trust between the leader and the led. It is a symbiotic relationship. If the other members of the team start to think that the team leader is incompetent and a bullshitter, the respect will start to erode.

Or, as Sir Stuart Rose puts it:

> If, after a while, you decide that going left was the wrong thing, tell people, 'I said left, but now I can see that I've made a mistake and now I am going to go right.' They will say, 'Fine', if you explain it. You can make a wrong decision if you give a good reason.

I think one of the quickest and bravest about-turns I have ever witnessed was executed by my former Asda colleague Archie Norman. He fired a new director of marketing on his first day of the job. Some leaders may have found such a rapid volte-face a huge blow, but Archie never saw it that way.

> In this particular case, I knew the person involved was an abrasive character, but I thought I was getting in a piece of grit in the oyster that would supercharge things and stir them up. He arrived in Leeds and had an induction programme which our HR guy set up. It was all quite informal as he went around the various departments to meet everyone. But, after he met his colleagues, many of them were coming to me and asking, 'This guy you recruited, what exactly is his role?' It just became apparent to me that it was not going to work. This person was, frankly, a bit full of himself and I realised culturally he just didn't fit.
>
> I thought, well, I could give him a chance, or decide now. I knew that if we parted company in six months' time the cost and embarrassment to me and the company would be much greater and the cost to him would be much worse too.
>
> At the end of that first day I got him round and I said, 'I've just

been reflecting on what I've heard in the day and you've had a chance to do the same. I just wanted to ask whether you think the best thing would be if you had never joined here?' He said, 'Well, you might be right, I am not sure either.' He didn't expect me to say what I said next.

I said, 'Well, if neither of us is sure there is only one thing to do, which is I'll pay your contract and as far as we are both concerned this never happened.'

He probably left in a complete daze, but actually it was the right thing for him because he never had to explain away a three-month failure on his CV. It was as if it had never happened. Plus, we looked after him financially.

Archie has no doubts at all that he did precisely what was required:

> It was the right thing for him and the right thing for us. All it required was for me to put a bucket full of egg on my face. What did everybody in the company think? They thought, 'Thank God he is gone.' What did they all think of me? They thought, 'Gosh, that was decisive.'

You can spot the really bad decision-makers because they never change their minds. Their refusal to engage with what is actually happening shows itself in their determination to plod on regardless of what is going on around them. They may even adopt the tactic so loved by politicians of resolutely refusing to admit to any error of judgement. Or when the evidence becomes overwhelmingly compelling they may try to foist the blame on some poor, hapless underling. Nobody is fooled.

BT's Ian Livingstone, who, as we saw earlier, is the embodiment of objectivity in decision-making, similarly knows when you have to change your mind:

> We put some money into developing a tablet device for the home. Then, right in the middle of it, Apple came up with its iPad. We agreed to stop our project and told the team to concentrate on applications and not the hardware. Our product was a good idea, it was in the right direction, but the market had completely changed.
>
> Life is like that sometimes. Move on.

Studying the evidence, learning the lesson

Things go wrong in business all the time. The important thing is to recognise it and put it right. Then, don't do it again.

Most of the time it is pretty obvious how, when and why you've screwed up. Think, for example, of the disastrous world-image tail fins British Airways introduced in 1997. Inexplicably the airline giant decided to turn its back on its traditional British image and feature all sorts of funky designs. Everyone hated it. Former Prime Minister Margaret Thatcher endeared herself to millions when she pointedly draped a handkerchief on the tail fin of a model 747, declaring, 'We fly the British flag, not these awful things.'

The lesson was learned. The entire British Airways fleet now boasts the Union Flag livery and I would be very surprised if that ever changes again.

The need for speed

The worst crime when things go wrong is to do nothing at all. The ostrich approach never helps. If anything, it will probably make things worse.

One of the most famous examples of this must surely be Mercedes Benz's original reaction when its new A-Class 'baby Benz' failed the so-called 'Moose Test' in October 1997. The car giant had invested $1.5 billion on the project and could scarcely believe it when Swedish magazine *Teknikens Vaerld* said the car had rolled over during its standard test that simulates the way a driver would swerve if a person – or moose – stepped into the road.

The car maker's initial reaction was completely unapologetic. One official told the media that the firm did not consider it necessary to comment 'just because somewhere in the world a car was rolled over'. Then, while stubbornly defending the safety of the A-Class, Mercedes publicly ridiculed the journalist who had conducted the test. For a brief while the focus switched to the possibility that the tyres were at fault. It was not until February 1998, following several more independent tests, that Mercedes finally bowed to the inevitable and recalled cars from the market. By that point, the press had had a field day. After all, when a strong and revered company trips up so badly, no news organisation could possibly resist.

In some cases changing your mind swiftly in the light of unfolding events can even be turned to an advantage. Back in 1985 Coca-Cola recovered reasonably swiftly because they decided to pull the plug on New Coke – and some have even claimed that all the publicity actually helped the company. More recently at the BBC, director general Mark Thompson similarly benefited from a public furore when the corporation announced their plans to close the digital radio station 6 Music at the end of 2011.

Mark's reasons for closing 6 Music were sound in financial and business terms – the brutal fact of the matter was that not that many people listened to it. As he recalls, 'We proposed shutting down 6 Music partly because when we surveyed people listening to it, about half of them said they wouldn't mind if we shut it down or not.' However, when the BBC's decision was made public it led to an outpouring of rage from listeners, trade unions, politicians and pop stars. In a short space of time, 6 Music doubled its listening figures.

It was at this point that Mark recognised that the original decision was no longer tenable and he moved swiftly to reverse it:

> Once it became a public talking point, it turned out that an awful lot of people felt very passionately about it. Then an awful lot more people started listening to 6 Music because of the publicity the row generated.
>
> I am absolutely prepared to accept that not everything you do is right and it is more often than not the public that prove you wrong.

However, in this case, an initial 'wrong' decision paid off handsomely. It might have been the cause of some embarrassment at the BBC, but this was temporary. 'At no additional marketing cost,' Mark says, 'we doubled the audience of the service.'

Not all changed decisions have to be 180-degree turns. In some cases, what is required is a slight shift in emphasis rather than a change in policy to get things back on track – particularly if, as often happens, the policy hasn't been executed quite correctly.

However, this only really goes for the smaller ones. Anyone who tells you that you can transform the wrong major decision with a tweak is either a liar or a miracle worker. Magic we can do. Miracles only have one owner. It is very dangerous to travel in hope and think that a minor shift here or there will correct something major which is clearly not right. It won't. You must go back to the beginning and look at it afresh.

It is up to a leader to judge how significant the decision is and whether or not it can be rescued with a slight adjustment, or if there is a need to go back to the drawing board.

In Ian Cheshire's case, he was able to get his attempts to conserve cash at the DIY group at the beginning of the credit crunch back on course with some stern words to the team after it got slightly out of hand:

> I had been so busy hammering people about working capital that some people misunderstood it and thought, 'Right, no stock.' Of course, that wasn't what I meant. What I wanted was stock that moves. You know, the stuff that we could resell and then pay for it later, as opposed to the pile of stock that won't move for 300 years but was paid for two years ago.

Here a readjustment in the face of the evidence was called for, not an abandonment of the original policy:

> We had to tell the team the story remained the same, we have not changed strategy, but this is what we actually wanted. Looking back we probably overdid it on how we emphasised the importance of chasing cash on some areas.

Avoiding the blame game

Admitting to mistakes is a culture that is led from the top, and it needs to cascade right through an organisation. If the lead decision-maker recognises that they will make mistakes, they have to recognise that others will, too. Indeed, they should actively encourage a culture where mistakes are known to be tolerated. Dalton Philips, Morrison's chief executive, even occasionally lets his team fall into the odd bear trap – to help them develop their skills.

> Sometimes I let people make what is clearly the wrong decision, because they have to learn. After all, if it is the smaller stuff, why not? People have to be taught how to use their judgement and wisdom to make the right decision. If they are overruled every time they'll end up never making one. They'll just keep coming to you to ask if they should do this or that.

Someone who's good will be feeling bad enough about their decision already. You don't need to rub it in. What you need to be concerned with is not so much why they missed their target or why they made that dodgy decision, as whether they really tried to hit the target or if they really believed that the decision they made was the best one on the basis of the evidence available. If you create a culture where everyone is not scared of losing, they always win.

News Corporation's James Murdoch takes a similar view, arguing that a culture of innovation and creativity in decision-making throughout the whole team is essential.

> We always think of decision-making here as a question not so much of trying to get everything right, but encouraging people

to make decisions. Their careers won't go forward if they don't make those decisions and take some risks. Taking this approach means we have to be tolerant of people making mistakes. If you encourage decision-making and encourage people to make choices and to stand up for those choices, then you have to be willing to accept that some of those choices are going to be wrong. Those people have to feel that it is OK to be wrong some of the time – but within reasonable risk parameters and not in a way that is going to be catastrophic for them or the company.

Taking risks is a lot better than not taking risks, especially if you have a reasonable record. It does mean, though, that course correction is a necessary skill.

Sainsbury's Justin King agrees:

I have only two rules. The first is that the person involved understands completely why they made that mistake. If they can explain to me that decision, and why it was a good decision at that moment in time, based on what they knew, I can't have a problem with them making that choice. If they took a decision that was cavalier in any way, then I have a problem with it.

The second rule is that they have to learn from their mistake and not do it again. The only really bad decisions are wrong decisions that are repeated.

There's another very good, practical reason for not going off the deep end every time someone makes a mistake. As Justin King explains, such an approach can backfire spectacularly:

I have never understood shooting messengers. If you do, guess what, they stop coming.

This is a key consideration. Once people are blamed for making mistakes, and are penalised for having the courage to own up to them, they will eventually stop admitting to them or even mentioning them. This frequently happens in companies that are becoming basket cases. The person at the top becomes ever more isolated in an alternative universe where no one tells them the truth of what is really going on. As their isolation grows, their decision-making becomes worse and worse.

Openness and honesty is everything. It's all about doing the right thing.

Part 3:
Seeing it Through

Chapter Eight
Having the Right People on Board

There's a great cartoon by Scott Adams that shows an office worker reading a note from his boss. 'Can anybody read the boss's handwriting?' he asks. 'This note is incomprehensible.' A colleague suggests that perhaps it says, 'The clients must be killed at once.' The first worker duly walks off to carry out this dubious order, at which point his colleague muses to himself, 'Or it could have said "*billed* at once"?'

The best decisions will always fall apart if you don't have the right savvy people on board to carry them out. Good companies require smart people – not necessarily scores of executives with PhDs or Harvard Business School MBAs, or even a handful of A levels, but people with what Archie Norman describes as 'native cunning'. It should be taken for granted that most people who get to any sort of senior position are clever, but they also need that crucial ability to cut through a problem and understand what needs to be done to solve it. Cleverness and intelligence are not the same thing.

It follows, then, that if you want great decisions and great execution, you need to be surrounded by the best people there are. That might seem blindingly obvious, but it's amazing how many senior people are clearly terrified to take on smart colleagues. One can only assume they're worried that they will be outshone.

Dalton Philips recalls a crucial piece of advice given to him early in his career:

> When I was 23 I worked for a store manager called Silvestro. He was pretty unforgettable because he was short, with a huge pirate moustache and an ego as big as a house. But, he spoke some great words of wisdom. One thing that has stuck with me all these years was when he said, 'Dalton, surround yourself with the best and then you will become the best.'

As Dalton goes on to say, you need guts to be able to do this:

> If you have masses of self-confidence you can do that and if you don't you can't. Being successful is all about finding those great people, then giving them their head and letting them run. Occasionally you may have to rein them in, but that is fine.

Much of the reason why we were able to turn things around at Asda in five years was because we placed a major focus on getting the best people we could. This was quite a challenge. After all, nobody wants to swim towards the Titanic. What's more, such was the grim state of Asda's finances that we couldn't afford to offer the sort of wage packages that other more successful companies were able to. And, of course, the brutal fact of the matter is that there are never limitless supplies of great people around.

All we had to offer was our vision of what we were trying to do and our enthusiasm about what we thought we could achieve given the chance. We could also demonstrate that we had entirely dispensed with the rigidly hierarchical structure so beloved of that period, so allowing smart people room to manoeuvre and make an impact. This proved sufficient to attract some of the smartest minds in retailing, people such as Justin King, Richard Baker, Andy Hornby and Andy Clarke.

This strategy, which was so key to making Asda the success it became, was based first and foremost on an understanding of what motivates talented people to join an organisation – and stay there. Archie Norman summarises this in the following terms:

> **What attracts the best people to join and makes them work harder is believing what they are doing is rewarding, though not just in a financial way. Work is a big part of people's daily life and most people work for more reasons than getting a daily crust. Their relation to a company isn't just the weekly pay cheque; it is the thought that they are a part of something valuable. They want to feel proud of what they do and to explain to people that where they are spending their working life is worthwhile. That is very different to 20 to 30 years ago.**

If talented people are looking for more than a good wage packet, then it follows that a well-run organisation will accommodate their ambition and aspirations. As Archie goes on to say:

A big part of this is getting rid of the hierarchy where in days gone by there was an automatic assumption that if you reported to someone they had legitimacy. The big boss came into the room and everybody metaphorically stood to attention. I know a lot of people say they have dispensed with this structure and I've heard many chief executives say they are completely non-hierarchical and single status, but it is just not the way they behave. Dispensing with the hierarchy is a very demanding model which requires continuous communication, consistent values and leaders to live those values.

In the modern workplace, all legitimacy should be earned. The way people work with others doesn't start with the assumption of status. Everyone begins with the premise that they are just the same, whether they are the marketing director or the checkout operator, and worthy of equal respect.

Companies need to understand this if they want to attract the best and keep them. Pace of work, commitment and motivation have now become extraordinarily important and it is something that has to be explicitly managed. Companies can manage this by creating a value system that people want to be part of. The accent on effective leadership and communication is much, much greater now because smart people are demanding it and have higher expectations. Leaders ignore that at their peril.

This approach was also deployed with considerable success some years ago by legendary businessman Gerald Fairtlough while at Royal Dutch Shell group. Gerald, who is sadly no longer with us, became chief executive of Shell Chemicals UK in 1975. At that time, command and control was pretty much the only way to get things done. Yet, Gerald argued that just because conventional hierarchy was hard-wired into the brains of the workforce he inherited, it didn't necessarily make it useful or productive.

Gerald was honest enough to admit that, contrary to the rigid rules of hierarchy as understood then, he didn't always know all the answers. His belief was that it was much better to talk to people throughout the company to arrive at the best possible, informed answer. However, he was also quick to point out that that didn't mean he had abandoned leadership. He was dispersing leadership throughout the organisation to give everyone a sense of purpose. In other words, once he had persuaded everyone to relinquish the old rules of hierarchy, and blindly depend on the next person up the ladder, it released an energy and enthusiasm that Shell had never previously had.

This technique requires a very delicate balance. Ultimately the person at the top has to take or sanction the big decisions. You can't have a free-for-all. On the other hand, if they want the best input into those decisions and the best new ideas, then leaders have to have the confidence to take on smart people and expect them to have their own views. Great leaders can do both. Bad leaders either ride roughshod over others or weakly defer to the last person to speak to them. It's an approach guaranteed both to produce poor decision-making and the gradual haemorrhaging of talented people.

Fresh thinking required

It's extraordinary how many companies, clearly crying out for someone talented to deal with a core area of their business, seem content to muddle through with what they have got. Indeed, in some cases, they seem happy to muddle through with what they haven't got, deciding, for example, that some major new venture or strategy can simply be divvied up among people who have no understanding of it. It's something that Carolyn McCall experienced for herself when she joined easyJet:

> When I joined easyJet, it did not have a marketing director. The last senior marketing expert the company had was David Magliano, who was a brilliant marketing director but left in 2003. I found this astonishing given how important it was to develop the brand in Europe. To me, marketing was a critical function in order to get a full understanding of the consumer there and we needed to be up at full strength in this department.
>
> The first thing I did after sorting out ops, was to bring in a heavyweight marketing consultant on an interim basis to do a brand audit and really work on what we should be doing with the brand in Europe. I also got him to help me find a UK marketing director.

Inevitably there was internal resistance. 'When someone comes in from the outside,' Carolyn says, 'people will already have their established territories and there will always be blockers.' Having brought in her expert, therefore, Carolyn also had to realign the structure of the organisation to deliver the new strategy, and marketing was part of that.

DECISION-MAKING LESSONS

› If you are going to do something that is not going to be liked, don't try to shroud it, cloak it, or obfuscate. People will see right through it and you lose trust.

› Consult and then listen. It won't just help in making the decision, but it will show you different ways to implement it too.

› Your team should know that they are part of the solution – they shouldn't just be waiting for problems to be solved for them.

Carolyn McCall, easyJet

Even when you do have the right people doing the right jobs, the injection of constant fresh thinking is essential. Andy Clarke's early moves when he took over as chief executive of Asda in 2010 are a classic instance of this. He was one of our first Asda hirings back in 1992, when we brought him in to run our development team. He then had a couple of brief stints outside the business at the clothing retailer Matalan and discount food chain Iceland, but he is ultimately Asda through and through. Consequently when he took on the top job he knew that he had to guard against allowing things simply to flow on the way they had before:

> Fresh eyes don't just have to belong to the chief executive. You need a team with enough fresh DNA to challenge the norm. When I took the job, I moved up from the COO position and could have moved everyone up behind me. There were certainly people

who were ready. But I decided also to bring in some people from the outside, who were completely different from me and would challenge my thinking. If I hadn't have done that I would only ever have implemented according to what we had always done – and sometimes we have got it wrong. Sometimes you need someone to come in and say, 'Here are the steps that are needed to move on.'

One particular decision that Andy made is concrete proof of the wisdom of this approach:

A case in point was our deal with [Danish discounter] Netto, where we ended up with 150 small stores. The idea was to trade them as smaller versions of our main supermarkets. However, one thing that was obvious to me thanks to my time at Iceland is that you can't run small shops as though they were a scaled-down superstore; you need a completely different model. If I had left it up to the people within the company they would have run a scaled-down model. So, I bought in someone from the outside who started with a clean piece of paper and built up a small store model from scratch.

You would expect successful entrepreneurs not to follow this approach. After all, it was their original vision that made success possible. But time and time again, you'll find that the successful ones actively encourage the influx of new blood and new thinking. The hotel chain owner Surinder Arora, for example, took the decision in 2009 to appoint an advisory board to the privately owned company, because he increasingly felt that he needed people to provide a fresh perspective:

My good old mum may not have been a qualified expert, but in my younger days in business while she was still with me, she always challenged me. Over the past few years there has been no one to challenge me and I could see that I needed that. I have now got a couple of non-executive directors who are there as a sounding board. I really appreciate the fact that they see things from a different angle. Their experience and expertise brings wisdom into the company which is really important now we have grown to the size we have.

As a privately owned company, we have always been able to make quick decisions. In the past, I have been able to say to my FD or MD, 'How much have we got in the bank? Let's go and buy X.' Now I am still able to buy something tomorrow, but I won't just do it by myself any more. I will sound off my MD, CFO and chairman just to make sure I am doing the right thing.

A lot of people might say, 'Isn't that worse? You used to be able to just make your own decisions.' But actually I now feel a lot happier. It feels like there is someone else looking at it from my side.

To move forward, you need the right team behind you and to find the right balance.

Obviously, the key word here is 'balance'. In a turnaround situation, when everything has to be re-examined, everything is also up for grabs. This was certainly the situation for me at both Asda and Royal Mail. But, if a company is well established and running smoothly, care must be taken not to ruin the existing, successful culture by swamping it with new people. Sir Stuart Rose neatly puts it:

It is like putting a kidney into someone's body. It can take it, but if you try to give it too much at once, say two kidneys, there might be a rejection process. That is why you have to get the tissue typing right. You have to get the right human being in. There are some people that you know from the minute you look at them are not going to fit into the business, no matter how qualified they are.

He goes so far as to put a figure on what is required:

All companies should be taking in around 10 per cent new DNA every year. We all need the benefit of fresh eyes, but if you bring too many in you will dilute the business, or you will cause chaos and upset.

DECISION-MAKING LESSONS
› The worst thing is not making a decision at all. Never sit on the fence, because you will just get very sore.
› Decisions in all organisations can be plotted on a line ranging between anarchy and control. Asda, in its history, has been high on anarchy. Ideally though, the best place is somewhere in the middle, possibly slightly left of centre into anarchy, so there is room for a few wild and wacky things.

Andy Clarke, Asda

Finding the right people

So how do you find the best people?

I'll freely admit that I've made bad hires. Recruitment is not an exact science and it's easy to get it wrong. The problem is that the interview process is basically an exercise in good acting, and, generally, the more senior the position, the better the perform-ance from the candidate. Time and again people have told me that they have made disastrous hires because the person who had a fantastic CV and came across so well in an interview behaved very differently once they got their feet under their new desks. This is inevitable from time to time. All you can do when that happens is to move swiftly to put things right.

There are, however, one or two tricks of the trade I have learned over the years. I now always work on the assumption that, once a candidate has been sent to see me, they have probably been through an exhaustive process to check their previous experience and whether they are up to the current job in question. They've probably done a plethora of psychological tests too. So, there is clearly no point in me going over all that again.

Instead, I spend time asking them about themselves, their fami-lies and interests. I ask them what they did at the weekend, who is their favourite newsreader, what was the best article they saw in the newspaper last week? I do this on the basis that it may be very easy for people to brush up on the latest business fads or marketing techniques, but it is a lot harder to be polished and put on an act when you are being asked about everyday life. It's hard to dazzle someone with business-speak if they've just asked you why you chose a retriever rather than a Labrador.

What you should be looking for is 'fit'. You want to know how this person will fall into the culture of your company. To do this you need to see how comfortable they are talking about the world at large. Once you see how they react to more unexpected questions, you can deduce how comfortable they are in their own space and most importantly whether they are a good fit for you.

Adam Crozier has an interesting approach to interviews, which he says he used to great effect when building his teams at the Royal Mail and ITV. His argument is that the best way to find out about someone's true character is to get them to discuss things that have gone badly wrong in their career. He doesn't mean asking that anodyne interview favourite, 'What are your weaknesses?' He knows as well as everyone else that most people will simply trot out a positive aspect of their career, dressed up as a weakness. With feigned embarrassment they'll say they always work too many hours a day, or are totally obsessed by getting a job done. No, what Adam wants to know about is the bits most of us like to bury quietly in our CVs. It is a trick he learned from his days as chief executive of the Football Association.

> I always remember Alex Ferguson telling me that he liked players that had been through a really bad time, because once they had been through it and come out the other end, they knew they could. That knowledge that you can overcome adversity makes anyone a stronger player.
>
> When I interview people I spend most of the time asking about the really horrible things that went terribly wrong. That is how you find out what people are really like. It is the easiest thing in the world to be able to run things or manage anything when everything is going great. What really matters is when it all starts going wrong, or when something needs fixing. That is

when people find out whether they can rely on you. I want to know if they can take the blows.

In many ways, if people are prepared to talk about the bad bits, that tells you something too. That is confidence. They have learned something. They went through it, it was difficult, but they know how to handle it now.

People only ever put in CVs the good bits about what happened at a company while they were there. Of course, the issue really is, 'Yes, but what did you do that made all the difference?' They'll say, 'When I was there the sales went up by 50 per cent.' 'Yes, that is great,' I'll say, 'but out of interest, what did you do that contributed to that? Were you leading that?'

The technology giant Google has a notoriously tough interview process, which is designed to check out how candidates cope when the pressure is turned up. There are various different rounds in the process, with each one getting progressively more complex. The questions don't require special knowledge about specific subjects, even though they focus on areas from problem-solving to algorithm development, to coding and analysis. What the interviewers are more concerned about is that their interviewees don't tie themselves in knots trying to find the 'single' way to solve a problem. They just want to know *how* the candidate tackles the tough ones. They are looking for confident people who don't get fazed by obstacles.

It's also important to recognise that there is always talent within the existing organisation that can be nurtured and brought on. Bringing in fresh thinking from outside is often the way to go, but sometimes people are too easily impressed by the external candidate. Because they have no history with the company, no one knows about the mistakes they have made: to all intents and purposes they walk on water. By contrast, the internal candidate suffers because everybody knows everything about them, warts and all. The decision is therefore made on partial knowledge – and that's a dangerous thing.

General Sir Mike Jackson is one who strongly believes in the virtues of growing internal talent. As he says, you then have years to observe people's strengths and weaknesses and nurture their skills. It is certainly a more reliable process than trying to assess someone's character, judgement and aptitude on the basis of a couple of interviews and a psychometric test.

> The army is a monopoly. If you want a 42-year-old brigade commander with proper military operational experience, training and education, you cannot go out there and buy one. You can only grow your own. Therefore, the time and effort that goes into growing our own is very considerable indeed.
>
> I don't see how you can do it any other way. How can you get a sense of what this guy would be like if the going gets rough and he or she has to dig a bit deep and make a difficult call? I'm not sure it is possible to do that on a basis of an hour's interview.
>
> When you are looking for qualities like judgement, which is something we very much look for among senior leadership, an opinion of someone's judgement can only be derived by seeing how they handle this or that conundrum over time. It is not something you can do instantly.

Former BUPA chief executive Val Gooding concurs:

> Despite what psychologists and recruitment experts will tell you, I don't believe you can really get to know a person from an

interview process in anything like the same way that you know someone you have already worked with. And if you trust that person, it's often worth taking a gamble on them even if they are not yet quite qualified to do the new job, because you know them well enough to be confident that, in time, they will deliver. That may sound counter-intuitive, but it is true.

DECISION MAKING LESSONS

› For the really tough calls, don't be in too much of a hurry. It undermines a chief executive's authority if they are seen to be regularly flip-flopping. Get all the information in first, because you will often make a better decision by waiting.

› Motivation is a very fragile thing. Consider how all decisions will play out with your senior team and be sensitive to the people implications of anything you do.

› While you are making a decision, draft in your head how you are going to express it to the team, the words you are going to use and the way you will communicate it. I have often found this exercise can either strengthen your resolve, or expose weaknesses in your argument.

Val Gooding, former chief executive, BUPA

One of the hallmarks of successful companies is that they're brilliant at attracting and then developing their own talent pool. This is not a passive process where you simply wait for good people to shine. It's a two-way process: potential stars show their talent and you then help them develop their careers.

Andy Clarke recalls the way in which he and a bunch of other very promising people were encouraged to take the next step in their early career at Asda:

> Back in 1995, my peer group was Justin King, Andy Hornby, Richard Baker and Ian McLeod. In truth we were massively over-resourced in the talent stakes, but that is what was needed in the renewal stage. One reason why the class of '95 was so strong was Asda did a huge amount of diagonal development, moving people out of functional expertise, to non-functional expertise and back again, operators into buying, and so on. I remember Justin, who was MD of Häagen-Dazs before he joined, running HR, private label, categories, frozen, bakery and an operating division all within a few years. In my own growing phase I did eight jobs in five years. That is what Asda was good at and it nurtured some formidable talents.

A measure of the success of any company in growing its own talent is, of course, when one of those people from the talent pool goes on to take the top job. This is what happened to Ian Cheshire, who had spent ten years at DIY conglomerate Kingfisher, including eight years as a board director, before finally being promoted to chief executive. He is acutely aware of the potential pitfalls here – as well as the advantages:

My pitch to the board was that they could either get someone who was completely from the outside who would say they were not interested in anything they had ever heard before because they were changing everything, or they could take an insider who could say, 'Yes I am from the inside but I have a completely different view of how I want to change things.' I assured them I was not there for the status quo. I actually thought things had to be done differently and said I thought I could double the profit. If an insider had come along and said, 'I think we can do 7 per cent a year better,' then that would hardly have been a change at all.

There is a role for a radical insider although I accept that the danger is that they will get the diagnosis wrong because they have always been told that this is the way things are. Looking at what had happened at Kingfisher, though, I was not sure how quickly an outsider could have understood what the problems were. An informed insider with a change mission and an agenda is possibly quicker off of the blocks and less likely to completely cock it up.

One of the most high-profile examples of a company continuously nurturing its own talent is Tesco. Sir Terry Leahy joined Tesco in 1979, after graduating from the University of Manchester Institute of Science and Technology. He started off as a marketing executive and rose through the ranks to be appointed to Tesco's board of directors in 1992. In 1997, by the time he was 40 years old, he had worked his way up to become chief executive.

In Sir Terry's 14 years at the helm, he delivered a shareholder return of 414 per cent, expanding the company into 12 countries around the world, and overseeing a four-fold expansion of the company's UK stores from 568 to 2,482. In the same period annual sales at Tesco increased 350 per cent from £13.8 billion to £62.5 billion, and operating profits rocketed from £774 million to £3.4 billion.

When it came to selecting a successor, Tesco promoted from within, naming international expert Philip Clarke as the man to replace Sir Terry. Philip has also spent his entire career at Tesco, joining the company in 1981 as a graduate trainee after studying economics at Liverpool University.

I spoke to Sir Terry Leahy a few weeks before he handed over in March 2011, just a couple of days after I had heard another retail chief executive privately speculate that once Sir Terry had left the remaining Tesco executives would be 'like rabbits in the head-lights', so used were they to taking direction from one powerful figurehead. His belief was that, having learned one way of doing things from Sir Terry, they would find it virtually impossible to think for themselves.

Sir Terry was, not surprisingly, having none of it. His view was that the culture of Tesco is so strong that it could never be based on just one man:

> **Tesco will be fine without me. It will be more than fine. The trad-ition in Tesco is that it has always had clear leadership and that will continue. Jack was a clear leader, Ian was, I was and Philip Clarke, my successor, will be. That part of it will always be there. In the end, the success or failure of Tesco will depend on what Philip and his team do. It won't depend on the fact that I have gone.**
>
> **Besides which, retail is such a busy business that within a week they will have forgotten I was here because they are always just thinking about the next day's sales.**

It's a measure of the strength and consistency of Tesco's vision, and its iron determination to stick to first principles, that it has been able to generate its own highly successful leaders.

Dealing with the wrong people

If finding the right people to make good decisions and execute them is crucial to an organisation's health and success, then the following is equally true: no company can afford to be complacent about weak performers.

They can be found at any level, but the ones who are most dangerous – the ones Justin King calls internal terrorists (see Chapter 1) – are generally found among senior executives and among the layer upon layer of middle management who appear utterly impervious to accepting a new way of doing things. Everything could be collapsing around them, but they'll still stick rigidly to doing all those things that contributed to the disaster while resisting anything that might put things right. They are often the leaders of the 'Business Prevention Squads', the permafrost that stops things happening in an organisation.

I think the time in my career when I was most aware of such people was when I joined Royal Mail. I remember a senior colleague coming to me just a week after he joined and telling me that he felt it was like working in the former Soviet Union. No one was happy with the situation, particularly the staff lower down the pecking order, but no one was prepared to do anything about it. One employee opinion survey which was taken shortly before I joined showed that less than 15 per cent of the staff felt valued by the company and 17 per cent claimed to have been bullied. (At Asda 95 per cent of colleagues said they felt valued.)

When you feel that you can't really trust what people at the top are telling you, do what I always do on these occasions: turn to people at the sharp end. Experience shows that it's those on the front line who have the clearest idea of what is wrong, even if they don't necessarily know how to put it right. They're the ones who are talking to customers and end-users, after all. Plus, they are the ones who end up cleaning up the mess made by nonsensical decisions from many of the head office 'experts' who were clearly anything but.

Speaking to the posties was a real eye-opener. I discovered that many of the technology and automation processes the Royal Mail had spent its money on did not work. No one at head office had bothered to mention this (or perhaps they didn't bother to find out) and clearly good money had been spent after bad for some time.

I also found that Royal Mail, like many companies these days, rightly prided itself on its positive recruitment philosophy, which welcomed people with disabilities. However, that welcome often came to an abrupt halt once new recruits started in the business. Some mail centres reported back a chronic bullying problem, but until then there was little structure in place to do anything about it.

In fact, I found that the gulf between the posties and those at head office was absolutely huge. They could have been working for different organisations. No one out in the sorting centres and post offices had even heard of the myriad of strategies being cooked up at head office, which I outlined earlier. More worryingly, they had no idea that the Royal Mail was losing so much money. Apparently, no one thought it was worth telling them about it.

Like me, Dyson's chief executive Martin McCourt believes that this is an area where you have to take swift action. If you don't fire fast, you are simply deferring a problem that won't go away and that could get out of hand later on.

> We are quicker than most when it comes to moving people out of the company if things aren't working. But we don't think it is ruthless. It is better for all parties to end it quickly.
>
> I always say to my senior team, 'Don't make the *decision* difficult. It isn't difficult. It is a difficult thing to *do*, but it should be a very easy thing to decide to do. Everyone should know what the criteria are: they know the signs of performance and under-performance. All you do then is put it all together and make a judgement. You need to use your instincts and not fall into the trap of convincing yourself that a bit of sticky tape can keep the situation together. All you will do is have a bigger mess to clear up later on.

Chapter Nine

Winning Hearts and Minds

'Followship,' says Lord Dannatt, 'is the flipside of leadership.'

You might think you are the great leader, but having got there if you look behind you and find there is no one there then it is a bit disconcerting. That is really why a good leader should make great efforts to know all his people and that they know him or her too. If they think that you are doing the right thing, and have the right approach, they will follow with a good degree of enthusiasm.

It is all a question of character and integrity. The subordinates will look at the boss and decide whether they like the look of that person. They will have a view on whether he is charismatic, an attractive character and whether they like what they see. More importantly they will decide the extent to which they trust their leader. If they like the look of someone they will probably follow them. If they really trust them, then they will follow them with a greater degree of enthusiasm.

If your integrity is high, you can have a high degree of confi-

dence that, even if other people may not agree with you, they can't really criticise you.

Time and time again, when you ask people what they admire in a leader they will say, 'integrity'. And if you want to ensure that major decisions are successfully executed, then Lord Dannatt's injunctions here are critical. It's not enough to have a great idea. You have to have the sort of personal qualities that will win other people over to it, too.

Integrity involves a range of qualities, but it's important to recognise what it doesn't include as much as what it does. First and foremost integrity is not about popularity. I am sure most people are familiar with companies that suffer from terminal niceness. It's all touchy-feely and high fives and everyone praising each other to the hilt at company get-togethers. Listen carefully though, and you'll hear the whispers when they get outside that reveal that, while no one is prepared to stick their neck out and say anything, quite a few are not really full square behind the company line. They just don't want to be seen to be the ones raining on the company parade.

'Niceness' for its own sake – or, indeed, 'likeability' – produces a conservative, risk-averse culture. Leaders who always avoid talking about the negatives, or make reticent decisions for fear of stepping on other people's toes, encourage an atmosphere of unreality. When suddenly resources are tight and markets are tough, the wake-up call will probably come too late.

People want their leaders to lead. They want to see decisiveness, a sense of clear direction and action, even if, sometimes, it is not always to their personal advantage. Doing something is a lot better than doing nothing, for all concerned. This is certainly the experience of Justin King, who told me a story of a potentially unsettling experience at the Sainsbury's Christmas party, which came just weeks after he had announced some severe job cuts in late 2004. Justin made sure he and the rest of the top team were there and highly visible, even though he could see they wouldn't be the most welcome of guests under the circumstances.

> It was a very lively event and I remember very specifically one guy coming up to me. He was a large lad and he said, 'Justin, I want to talk to you. As I am one of the 750 people you fired and I am going tomorrow, I won't have the chance to talk to you again.'
>
> He then said; 'I just want to shake you by the hand and wish you well. Obviously, I am devastated that I am going, but we all knew it needed doing.'

There's a further danger with courting popularity for its own sake. People who try to be friends with everyone end up being friends with no one. Sooner or later you'll have to make a decision that someone somewhere won't like. If you've always been straight with your colleagues, they might not like a decision, but they'll probably live with it. If you've been falsely pally with them though, they'll feel betrayed. No one likes to work with a tyrant, and I abhor bullying in the workplace, but pretending that you're everyone's friend does no favours, either to you or to others.

As Sir Stuart Rose puts it:

> Being a boss is not as sexy as people think it is. Being a boss means sometimes making yourself unpopular, or cutting across

what appear to be the prevailing truths, or sacking people, or cutting costs, or changing things. People hate change, but if you don't change things, things don't move forward.

Only one person can make a decision. By definition, if you have more than two people in the room, you are going to start having two different views. You are never going to please everybody. At some point you have to listen, distil, decide and make the decision. If there are ten people in the room, four of them are not going to agree with you and six people are. You have to say, I have listened to what it is you have to say but this is my view and we are going to do this and they have to come with you.

That is why leadership is lonely and why it's tough.

This is certainly something experienced by Adam Crozier during his tenure as chief executive of the Football Association, the governing body of the English national game. But, despite taking the job with both eyes open, nothing could have prepared Adam for the criticism heaped on his head when he appointed the Swede Sven-Goran Eriksson as England manager in early 2001. The fans, the media and even some of his own colleagues were, it seemed, not ready to accept the first ever foreign manager of the England team.

A lot of people were very unhappy and made their feelings very clear to me. I also got a postbag full of hundreds of death threats sent by 'fans'. It was pretty hairy for a while. The point about decisions like this though is: you have to do the right thing, even if it is more difficult. Yes, you are going to get an avalanche of grief for doing it, and a lot of it will be very personal grief, but you can't afford to be distracted by getting worried about whether everybody likes you.

The whole point of leadership is making the tough calls and earning the respect through that. It's not about whether people like it or not.

In a similar way, BBC director general Mark Thompson is constantly under pressure from a range of sources, from internal views on how things should be done, to conflicting tastes of viewers, to constant scrutiny from the media. He knows, however, that he simply can't please everyone all the time:

> The BBC is full of smart, super-sharp, very articulate and very bolshie people. It is teaming with debate and argument. What everyone understands though is that the success of the BBC depends on our ability to serve the public. But pleasing all of the people all of the time is not what the public want. People accept that there are going to be some great things on the radio and television to suit them, but also they accept that the BBC should be making lots of programmes that they would not like to listen to and may even detest.
>
> We run a big restaurant. It is a restaurant to which everyone in the entire country goes and not everyone is going to like every-thing in the menu. It would be a slightly dull restaurant if everyone came in and found that there was nothing new – poached chicken for all! There have to be some strong flavours even though they won't be to everyone's taste. Knowing this is what makes the BBC strong.

DECISION-MAKING LESSONS
› You often don't have quite enough
  information, but that is the reality of
  life. Work out when you know as much
  as you reasonably need to know and
  then make the decision. Don't delay.
› No one has a 100 per cent record of
  making good decisions. If you tried to, it
  would make you completely risk
  adverse.
› The big enemy of clear-cut decision-
  making is tying yourself in knots and
  thinking everything is complicated and
  impossible. It rarely is.

Mark Thompson, BBC

Never shy away from telling your team what you think. They might not always want to hear it, they might not like you for saying it, but that doesn't mean that you should be prepared to pull your punches. And don't be afraid to use the occasional shock and awe tactic to produce the reaction you want.

At one company I was involved with, for example, we had to deal with a problem that kept occurring over and over again. At this company, we held a monthly meeting for the senior team which ran for four hours; it gave an opportunity for everyone to talk about their figures, how they were doing and what they were aiming for over the next four weeks.

At our first meeting, one particular team told me that their forecasts for the rest of the year were down. We discussed what needed to be done, and they went away to get on with it.

The next month, they came back and told me that, yet again, they couldn't meet their forecasts. By now I was getting irritated. But I decided to bite my lip, and used the best part of the meeting to tell them and show them exactly what had to be done to recover the situation.

One month on in the same meeting room the entire team was sitting there, ashen-faced. Again, they said, forecasts would have to be cut.

By now, irritation had turned to anger. 'Well, that's it then,' I said, standing up and walking to the door. 'End of meeting. You guys can all go away and work out exactly what to do. That's not my job and I refuse to talk about it a moment longer. You can come back in here on Monday morning to tell me what you are going to do. And I don't ever want to be in a situation again where you come in here with a forecast that is going backwards and you give no indication that you have a plan to sort things out.'

At which point I said goodbye and walked out of the door.

On Monday, the team returned with a plan and put it into action. It worked and they stopped having to reduce their forecasts.

I may not have won a popularity contest on that occasion, but I did get my message across. And the fact that things then improved demonstrated that I was right to have been angry. I'm sure there were one or two future chief executives or chairmen in that team, and I suspect that one day they will find themselves behaving exactly as I did.

Integrity doesn't involve seeking popularity, then. But it does demand total honesty and transparency. Paradoxically, this is particularly important when things aren't going too well and your natural reaction is to lock yourself in your office and not talk to anyone while you get on with figuring out what to do. Barclays' chairman Marcus Agius reckons that a classic mistake most companies make is to go very quiet just at the moment they need to explain what's going on:

> When a situation is fast-moving, to be inclusive and transparent is vitally important. Things that go wrong get worse when you don't have access to lots of different points of view. Including people makes the whole thing a bit more time-consuming, but it is amazing what you can do if you have to. If you have access to a number of different points of view you greatly reduce the risk of key people squirting away in another direction and setting up different camps with a different agenda. Sink or swim, you are in it together. It is a collective thing.

Shutting everyone out is dangerous for two reasons. First, a bunker mentality descends and decisions are made that are ever further at odds with what is actually going on. Secondly, key people in the organisation, who should be helping and supporting at this crucial moment, feel totally cut out of the loop. This can have serious long-term repercussions. As Marcus says:

> Very often in a crisis people say they can't be bothered to tell everyone everything; it is just too difficult. You get a little clique of the chief executive, the chairman, the finance director and maybe a couple of advisers. They close the door and sit down together for a private chat and things happen. Suddenly close colleagues who were until yesterday important are disempowered and demoralised. They know important and earth-shattering things are happening, the future of their company and

the future of their livelihood is being discussed and determined, yet they don't know what is going on.

Their subordinates turn to each other and say, 'What is happening?' For those who are normally in the loop to say 'I don't know' is not good enough for anyone.

I hasten to add that doesn't mean that if things are tough, openness requires that the person at the top should adopt the poise of a French aristocrat on the way to the guillotine. But you do need to be positive.

Of course, optimism involves a degree of window-dressing. To that extent you could argue that it's difficult to be both optimistic and completely open. There's a balance to be struck here. It's certainly true to say, however, that without a healthy dash of optimism most leaders would be unable to lead – leaders are, after all, 'dealers in hope'. As in everyday life, you can either panic when things look bad, convince yourself that it will only get worse whatever you do and do nothing, or you can pick yourself up, believe that things can get better and make the best out of the hand you've been dealt. I've always tried to follow the latter path. Nothing is ever perfect – to be honest I don't think I'd like it much if it was – so you do the best you can.

That said, people who are over-optimistic, to the point where they are out of touch with reality, are very dangerous. This is particularly so at the top of an organisation. And it's particularly so in tough times. False optimism, or travelling too much in hope – as I call it – implies a lack of grip. Next to a sense of direction, a strong grip is the most important characteristic a leader can bring to an organisation. You want to look up to the stars, but you need your feet firmly planted on the ground.

For Archie Norman, used to turning around companies others might not touch with a bargepole, such thinking is second nature:

> You have to accept that in business you never know from the outside what you are going to find until you look under the carpet. The golden rule is that when you look under the carpets, or open the cupboards and the skeletons come tumbling out, it is always worse than expected. It will carry on getting worse too, for at least six months.
>
> I always say to the people I bring in, 'I know I sold you a false prospectus, but I had to get you to join.' I know that, without exception, they will not be impressed by what they find, because I never am either.
>
> Looking on the bright side, experience shows me that there is a wallow curve and it always follows pretty much the same pattern. People arrive with high expectations. In the first week they will be impressed by some things, but their eyebrows will be raised by others. In the second week they will start to feel a bit worried about what they are finding. By the third week they will be completely appalled. Then, everything will carry on like this for at least six months, with the new person becoming increasingly frustrated by finding it more and more difficult to get things happening. But then, almost overnight, it does turn. It really does. The catalyst is getting enough good people on board to start things moving. First they are pioneers on their own, then they form platoons, and then things happen. Sometimes the false prospectus is justified.

Keeping it simple

Consider this candidate for a Golden Bull award from the Plain English Campaign in 2010. Worryingly, it comes from a business school.

> This new programme reflects the need for a more holistic perspective on risk as well as specialisation in discrete areas of risk management. It views organisations as complex structures interacting with one another and with the wider system, and with people being a component of both. Its core courses address concepts of globalisation of risks and the super structure necessary to manage them; complexity and diversity of new classes of emerging risks; system-wide responses under conditions of uncertainty, and resilience as a mechanism to enhance a systems ability to manage unknown risks.

Ah. Gobbledygook.

How much did you understand? More importantly, how much will you remember in an hour's time?

For the person at the top, it's all about keeping things simple, and that includes explaining strategy and decisions. This is not about patronising people. It's about helping them understand what it is you want to do, keeping it fresh in their minds, acting on it and then communicating the message to others. It ensures continuing focus. And you do it in plain words: '*Sun* speak'.

Once, for example, I chose the rock documentary *It Might Get Loud*, by film-maker Davis Guggenheim. The film explores the history of the electric guitar, focusing on the styles of three rock heroes: Jimmy Page, the Edge and Jack White. What had really struck home about this film was how all of these musicians had created their own very distinct guitar sound, even though they were essentially all playing the same instrument. My point to the team was that, actually, that is what we are trying to do. If you are in food retail, you have shops and you sell food. That means that every grocer has essentially the same instrument. The trick is for each to find its own unique sound. I asked everyone for their thoughts on how to make our business into the equivalent of the unique sound generated by Jimmy Page, or the Edge, or Jack White.

Back in my Asda days it was clear who had what sound. We had 'Asda price', our low price promise. Tesco was similarly rock solid in sticking to its 'Every little helps' value message, aiming to be the best at understanding their customers, meeting their needs with a wide range of food and non-food products, all at an affordable price. Morrisons had carved out a niche for preparing more fresh food than anyone else and Sainsbury had honed the quality message. In fact, at that time, Safeway was the only major group without a distinctive sound. That's why it eventually got taken over and disappeared from the market. Quite simply, it never managed to make its guitar sound different.

It is always so much more effective if you talk to people in these terms rather than saying something like, 'Let me talk to you about perfection' or 'How do you think we can improve this or that?' By getting my team to think about what we are all trying to achieve in the context of the rock documentary *It Might Get Loud*, everyone went away and thought, I get that.

Never miss an opportunity to reinforce the message, even if you're away from the business. Draw inspiration from all sorts of sources to come up with stories and analogies to ensure that decisions you've made or strategies that have been agreed on don't seem abstract to those you want to buy into them. It makes communication more interesting and memorable.

One thing I always do is to take an unusual book with me on my annual holiday and use it to try to generate some different thoughts and insights for the business. My thinking is that sometimes to see inside you need to step outside for a while and, for me, going on holiday is a little bit of stepping outside. It might be a business book that I read or something apparently completely unrelated. On holiday in Mexico, for example, I read *The Gamble: General Petraeus and the Untold Story of the American Surge in Iraq, 2006–2008* (Penguin, 2010). From this, I derived my very own 'Gamble: Mexican Memoirs' that I shared with my team. At the core of the book, I felt, was a distinction between being 'good' and being 'effective'. If you've chosen your team carefully, they should all be technically good at what they do, just like highly trained combat soldiers. But that doesn't necessarily make them effective in the campaign as a whole. Good teams see the bigger picture – they see beyond the nitty gritty of their own roles. *The Gamble* provided a concrete example of a key lesson for business.

The email I sent read as follows:

From: Allan Leighton
Subject: 'Gamble' Mexican Memoirs

It's been a tradition of mine, in taking more than 4 days' holiday, to read a book that 'makes me think', then write a note that captures some of the more salient points of that book and make them relevant to the business.

The book I read is called *The Gamble*. It's written by Thomas E. Ricks, a Pulitzer Prize winner, and is the story of General

David Petraeus and how he turned the fortunes of the US Army in Iraq around by what has become known as the 'Surge' strategy.

Basically, he doubled the number of troops, made them live in and around the people, and made the first priority of the US in Iraq to protect the people.

Prior to his appointment the first priority had been 'Kill the insurgents; to hell with the people'.

In essence it's a book about leadership, hence the connection to what we do . . . As always it underpins that leadership and running anything is about 'Planning', 'People', 'Choices'.

Planning

'The strategy was a hope posing as a plan' – Petraeus's view of what was happening in Iraq.

'There are two kinds of plan: those that fail and those that might just work' – Petraeus's view of his plan

It's useful for us to reflect on our strategy three years on. My view is that most of it still stands today and that it has stood the test of time. . .

But, as with Petraeus, 'everything takes longer than you think it's going to take' and things are often 'slow turning'. Our IT programmes I believe will follow this line. . .

People

Petraeus got the best people he could to do the work, ignored rank and tried to get 'new officers', because those he inherited were 'executing what they know' the old way. In his words, 'the Army is in worse shape than you think' . . . 'A lot of guys became afraid to fail'.

All the above has many parallels for us ... we must get more new talent and we must move our talent through quickly and give them the key roles...

Choices

There is a chapter in the book called 'Gambling on a shitty hand'. It's about making choices when you don't have many options, if any.

'Just because the odds were bad didn't mean there wasn't a better choice available.'

We have had a few of these, and will have more to come. We should identify them exactly as this, and not chew on them for too long.

I'd like us to reflect on this note, meet up and chat about it...

Great organisations know how to communicate ideas like this to their teams. And this is when, as I've said before, good execution becomes a habit rather than an act. Many leaders I admire are brilliant at this. Among them is Superquinn founder Feargal Quinn, who has always excelled at it and reaped the reward. Here, for example, he describes how he saw Superquinn staff embodying the chain's customer service values on a day when disaster struck:

One of the moments I am most proud of in the history of Superquinn came when my wife Denise and I were away at a meeting of the Food Marketing Institute in Switzerland. Ironically, the topic under discussion at the first session of the day was crisis management, when there was a knock at the door and a secretary came in to say there was an urgent phone call for me. It turned out

that our main supermarket in Sutton, Dublin, which also happened to be the site for Superquinn's headquarters, was on fire.

I immediately took steps to race back. Unfortunately, thanks to a series of mishaps, I missed my flight. By the time I got back to Dublin in the late afternoon, the supermarket and our head office was a smouldering pile of ash.

I was, of course, momentarily speechless. How could we carry on now? Then, bit by bit, my team revealed to me what had been going on while I had been struggling to return.

One colleague had opened a caravan at the hotel across the road to take orders from customers and set up a delivery service from one of our other supermarkets. Another had set up an agreement with the city's toll company that anyone driving to any of our other supermarkets across the nearby bridge wouldn't have to pay the toll. Another was handing out tickets for a free train to get customers to different branches.

Meanwhile, the executive team were already in touch with our insurance companies, as well as local builders and planners to find out how quickly we could get up and running again. They had also contacted our long list of suppliers and told them that all our records were destroyed so we had no idea what we owed them. They were all reassured that we were going to pay them whatever they looked for.

I could hardly believe that all of this had been done in such a short time and while this terrible fire was raging. I realised then that this was all due to the empowerment my team felt. I had always followed a policy of concentrating on what I did best and delegating the rest to my team. Everyone felt excited and involved and could share in my deep-rooted commitment to make the best of things for our all-important customers.

You can't please all the people . . .

That's how things are and should be when a company is on top form and communication is flowing. But, of course, it's not always like that. There are some occasions when, however much you seek to explain the message, you come up against a brick wall.

Carolyn McCall experienced this at first hand when she was chief executive of the Guardian Media Group (GMG) and was grappling with what changes needed to be made to ensure the group's survival in the modern media world. With the group suffering crippling losses of £100,000 a day, there was a need for urgent action. Two key parts of GMG's strategy going forward were the move over to the digital platform (which would lead to substantial job losses) and an alliance with private equity firm Apax to shake up the media group's portfolio of titles. In two deals in 2007, GMG sold Apax a 49 per cent share in Trader Media Group, publisher of *Auto Trader* and GMG's biggest cash generator. The pair then worked together, spending £1 billion acquiring Emap Communications, with its stable of business-to-business publications.

Carolyn found that while the National Union of Journalists (NUJ) understood the need for redundancies in reshaping the media group's digital functions, they were resolutely against any sort of cooperation with private equity.

> Commercially both parts of the strategy were absolutely the right thing to do and the board and the trust utterly agreed and believed in it too. But, despite the fact that I made it clear we were in a struggle for survival, I knew I would never win over the NUJ when it came to anything to do with private equity. They were prepared to work with me over the job cuts, but were dead

set against the principle of private equity. We made huge efforts to share with them all the information we had and to disclose the real challenges of the digital world. It did not matter what I said though, how rational I was with them, I could not persuade them of my case.

In situations such as this, you have no choice but to hold your nerve while you continue to communicate what it is you want to achieve. As Carolyn says, 'You have to be very calm, very patient and explain everything.' But as she adds, 'I never gave up but, at some point, you have to say, "Actually, there is not a lot more I can do." They had to accept that this was the way to solve the problem.'

I have experienced many stand-offs in my career, and on most occasions, having been at pains to explain why I was doing what I was doing, I was eventually forced to take pretty tough action. At Loblaw in Quebec in 2010, we were faced with a union connected to one of the distribution centres demanding huge pay rises for the team that worked there. When we told them that it was not possible in the current climate, they announced that they would go on strike.

Negotiations became increasingly fraught to the point where I felt there was no room for further discussion. We therefore took the decision to move products to other distribution centres bit by bit, so that by the day industrial action was due to start there was nothing left. We then locked the union out of the empty warehouse.

They were furious. A picket was mounted for a week. One week then stretched into two. Eventually the union recognised that we weren't going to change our mind and they announced that they would return to work. By this time, however, I felt we had reached the point of no return. We told the union that we would be closing down the distribution centre permanently, and that's exactly what we did.

At the Royal Mail one deeply problematic issue I faced was bound up with the culture. There were a handful of mail centres where sexism, racism and bullying were rife. So long had this been allowed to continue that it had become almost part of the culture. In fact, instead of facing up to it, making it clear that such conduct was unacceptable, and then nipping it in the bud, previous management had done little to stop the epidemic spreading. I therefore visited each centre involved and explained to people there that if we ever saw or heard about this behaviour again, we would close the place down without a second thought. I suspect they didn't believe me, because not much seemed to change. It's not hard to guess which centres topped the list when, shortly afterwards, we made a decision to streamline the organisation.

And the end result? The Royal Mail is not one of those bodies that is going to be fixed overnight. It really is a ten-year programme. There are simply too many interest groups and too much political capital involved. However, the initiatives put in place are delivering bit by painful bit. The organisation *is* being streamlined and made more efficient. The current government has been brave enough to do what previous ones should have done and looked at privatising it. How much better it would have been, and how much easier for all concerned, if everyone – including past governments – had been prepared to accept the inevitable from the outset. As I said earlier, when an organisation is really in crisis, the solutions are generally obvious to everyone – except, sadly, those in a position to help implement them.

As Moya Greene, Adam Crozier's successor at Royal Mail says, you have to engage actively in an attempt to win hearts and minds, but you simply cannot afford to back down. If you do so, you'll simply store up trouble for later.

> I always say, 'I will talk to you any time you want, on any day, Sunday, Monday, it doesn't matter to me. Call me. But on this day, in three months' time, that is it. We are going ahead.' Then the day comes and they say, 'We are not ready. We haven't done this and we haven't done that.' I say, 'Well, I'd just like to remind you that the first time we met we said this was the day we were going to go ahead.'

Chapter Ten

Communicating the Message

It was August 2010 and Andy Clarke was a few days into his new job as head of Asda. He had already decided what the company's strategy should be: to recover the number-two spot in the market by overtaking Sainsbury's. He had also decided how to achieve this: by improving food value and quality. He had, in other words, done exactly what a good decision-maker should do. He had identified a goal and outlined a way forward to achieve it.

All was going well until he embarked on the exhausting round of media interviews that always punctuate a new leader's first few weeks in the job. On one day alone he spoke to ten journalists, some face to face and some on the telephone. The message he gave them all was the same positive one: Asda would improve its market position and offer the customer a better deal at the same time. In one interview he emphasised, 'I'm very passionate about food values and food quality.' He also conceded, 'It's something we haven't spent enough time talking about or working on.' You can imagine his horror, then, when he opened the papers the following morning to find a banner headline that read: 'New boss admits supermarket's food isn't up to scratch.'

It was described by some as Andy's 'Ratner moment' – that instant when complete openness backfires horribly, just as it did for Gerald Ratner back in April 1991 when, in an unguarded moment during a speech at the Institute of Directors, he said that some of the items on sale in his shops were 'total crap'.

When you get to the end of the chapter you will see that this is not the case, but it nicely encapsulates the issues involved when you come to communicating your decisions to a wider audience. You have to be open. (I strongly believe that it is not only morally wrong to hide things, but tactically stupid: you get found out and no one trusts you again.) You also have to get your message across. (You can't say one thing inside your organisation and something altogether different outside.) But miscalculate even slightly and things can go very wrong.

It may be no consolation to Andy, but Justin King at Asda rivals Sainsbury's had a similar experience back in 2004. At this time, the grocer, once the industry leader, was in pretty bad shape. Tesco's lead was virtually unassailable; Asda had sailed past Sainsbury's to win the number two slot. There had been three profit warnings and a share price that underperformed rivals by 23 per cent.

Twelve weeks after he joined, Justin delivered Sainsbury's first quarter results and trading statement to a group of very cynical analysts and journalists. 'We know it has been another bad quarter,' he recalls saying, 'but we are starting to understand the company and will be back in three months' time to tell you what we are going to do.'

The reaction?

I got my head kicked in. I sat there thinking, 'What is going on here? These are not my numbers, I am trying to be positive and engaged and they are just kicking my head in for the sake of kicking it in.' That for me was quite an epiphany, because I realised that it wasn't actually my head they were kicking in, it was the company that was being kicked. I was the lightning conductor for that because I was the chief executive, but it made no difference that I had only been there for 12 weeks.

Justin weathered the immediate storm and felt he had learned an important lesson:

I realised that there were three key communities that I had to get in the same place, at the same time. Colleagues that work in the company, the customers that shop in our stores and the commentators, be they journalists or analysts, or others.

The night before we announced our 'Making Sainsbury's great again' strategy, we did a conference in Birmingham with all the top 1,200 people and went through all of the plans. The last thing I said to them was, 'Tomorrow morning I am going to be talking to the other communities, our commentators and our customers and your challenge is very simple. Every single colleague in the company has to hear this from you, their boss, before they hear it from a commentator or a customer. In simple terms, that means that by the time the *Evening Standard* has hit the newsstands, you have got to have communicated making Sainsbury's great again to your colleagues.'

The next day, while I was doing the City and media presentations, and all the radio and TV interviews, we had 1,200 people making sure that our version was communicated to our colleagues.

All the while that Justin was working through the back-to-basics 'Making Sainsbury's great again' strategy, which focused on such fundamental tasks as keeping the shelves fully stocked (something the chain had really let slip), he ensured that his team out in the stores were constant cheerleaders backing up everything Sainsbury's achieved.

I'm not going to pretend that balancing the interests of employees, customers and commentators is easy – or that satisfying them is always possible. But there are a few basic, common-sense rules that I always seek to apply.

Words have sharp edges

Language is powerful and emotive. If you get it even slightly wrong, then however sound the vision you may have, all people will remember is what you actually blurted out when you were trying to articulate it. That means that before you say anything publicly or commit a statement to paper you do need to think carefully about your audience and the impact your words may have.

This is particularly so these days when there's no guarantee that internal communication will stay that way. Witness the experience of Nokia's new chief executive Stephen Elop, who in February 2011 made a highly sensitive speech to his team – also reprinted on the firm's internal blog – warning that the company was standing on a 'burning platform' facing raging fires on multiple fronts. He went into detail about those threats and concluded that his company was not fighting with the right weapons. Unfortunately, Elop's words were leaked for all the world to see. His fears were real and he was right to raise them. The way in which he expressed himself, however, was, to put it mildly, unfortunate and became a distraction.

In fact it's now so easy to blurt out your thoughts that they can be halfway around the world before you've have had time to think them through properly. James Murdoch, who is a great fan of blogs and message boards when it comes to finding out what customers really think, also recognises that in unskilful or careless hands they can prove deeply problematic:

> I have been following a lot of journalists and commentators tweeting and blogging about News Corp. I am constantly amazed at the extent to which professional people seem willing to tweet their innermost thoughts at 2 am. They've been out to dinner, they've had a drink and then they are on Twitter. It is just madness. You have to have rules about your engagement in these areas.

I actually find online forums very useful and make sure that all blogs and tweets about my companies are constantly monitored. The reason is that if anything goes awry, the first place you'll generally find out about it is online. As a rule of thumb, bloggers highlight things first these days, then the press.

Although British Airways did not win plaudits for the way it handled the PR disaster that surrounded the botched opening of Heathrow's Terminal 5 in 2008, it seems to have learned a lesson or two since. During the recent cabin crew dispute, which blighted the airline for nearly two years, chief executive Willie Walsh turned to YouTube to appeal to both passengers and the media. Shedding his tie and appearing relaxed and casual, he thanked his customers for supporting the airline, saying, 'It's great to see people sticking with BA', and adding, 'We promised we would keep British Airways flying and that's exactly what we've done.' He refused to be cowed by the union rhetoric that dozens of aircraft were parked at Cardiff, saying with a shrug, 'We have a world-class maintenance facility there. That's why.' His calmness in the face of the apparent crisis and his simple yet powerful words, defused a situation that could have turned into a disaster for the airline.

You can't hide; you mustn't hide

I have never understood why even businesses that are good at communicating with their teams in private are often shy in public. Even if things aren't going the way you want them to, you have to be out there talking to people. In fact I'd go so far as to say that you should do this *particularly* if things aren't going the way you would like them to.

Take an intractable act-of-God problem – for example, the heavy snow in December 2010 that brought Heathrow Airport to a standstill. Having spent some time living and working in Canada, I am no stranger to snow, and lots of it, and have seen that countries can carry on working as normal even through the harshest winters. However, I also recognise that the sheer quantity of snow that fell in a very short space of time at Heathrow was such that any country would have struggled to cope with it.

This, then, is one of those 'It's bad, but there's not much we can do about it' situations which no one wants to be faced with. But just because there's not an easy answer doesn't mean that you shouldn't engage with people. If you don't it looks as though you don't care. What's more, you leave the door open for self-appointed experts to come up with their own views of what should be done and winning the argument, not because they're right, but because you're not there to tell how it really is.

I have to say that when I think back to the disruption at Heathrow my criticisms of BAA are not that they couldn't wave a magic wand and solve the problem – after all, no one could have done that – but that they opted for an information vacuum. In my experience, when there's an information vacuum, chaos rushes in to fill the void. Had key people gone out to stand on the tarmac next to the planes and explain the situation, there might at least have been some public recognition of the challenges involved, particularly if this had been done not in corporate speak but in concrete terms that everyone could relate to. Something along the lines of: 'I know people are getting frustrated, but let me tell you this. In most people's gardens there's around a quarter of a tonne of snow. This aeroplane has got 50 tonnes of snow surrounding it and we have 500 planes parked at Heathrow. We're working on it but we're not going to resolve it overnight.'

You can see this sort of approach being taken by people like Stephen Hester at RBS the whole time. He is running a company that has experienced major problems. It's in a sector that is currently unpopular with many. And turning it around involves making decisions that are inevitably not going to be universally popular. It would be tempting to keep in the shadows, but Stephen's approach is to accept the challenges publicly and engage with the arguments to get his views across. Take the contentious issue of bonuses, for example:

> **The starting point to my argument is that any organisation has to be able to attract and retain talented people. Talented people**

need to be engaged on many levels. But, one is that you pay them fairly and paying people fairly is a relative game. It is relative to what they could otherwise do and the particular market in which they compete. Our first duty is to be clear that our employment proposition, to exist at all, must be competitive. That doesn't mean we throw money at people though.

We have to find out how to bring the outside world with us, when it is much easier for the outside world to pick up scape-goats. Sometimes you can't win, but you have to keep trying to make progress.

Overall, by openly and unapologetically explaining precisely what he is seeking to achieve, he believes that he can gradually help move the debate about banks on and achieve a more balanced view of their function and obligations:

Of course, there can be short-term conflicts, just as there are in any companies with customers. Your customers would like more for less, and the government would like more tax. But, although it is clear that the banking industry needs reform and is reforming radically, it is also clear that the world needs banks. Economies cannot be successful and prosperous without banks also being successful. There is an interdependence that, when we all get into calmer waters, everyone will recognise. There are limits to which you can beat these things up and still have the positive benefits that the banks give to society.

It is an underlying hard fact that the job of people in respon-sible positions is to keep returning to that reality and explaining it, so that things can return to equilibrium.

DECISION-MAKING LESSONS
› There are two categories of difficult decisions. In the first, you will be absolutely sure that the decision is right, but know that the consequences will be difficult and unpleasant. In the second, you do your best to get them right, but are not completely certain you've made the right choice.
› For the category of decision where there are difficult consequences, the skill is in how you administer them.
› For the second category, you have to do the best you can, using as much available information within the time constraints presented to you.

Stephen Hester, RBS

It's not a beauty contest

Explaining why you have made the decision you have should never be a plea for first prize in a beauty contest. That way madness and future indecision lie. You're never going to please all the people all the time.

This is particularly so at companies with a high public profile which people feel that in some way they 'own'. I certainly found this at Royal Mail where everyone I spoke to had a view. Lorraine

Heggessey, who spent many years at the BBC in senior roles that included two years as head of children's television and five years as controller of BBC One, had a similar experience. As she found, the BBC, like the Royal Mail, is one of those British institutions that invite love and criticism in equal measure:

> Most people, if they are a lawyer or whatever, can go to a dinner party and nobody really knows how good or bad they are at their job, still less do they have a view. In my case, whether I was at the school dropping off the kids, or at a dinner party, or on holiday, everybody I met would have a view on the programmes of my channel. Plus, of course, the things that they will zoom in on were the things that they personally don't like, or on any of the decisions that I made that they didn't like. So, there is the added element that whatever you do, you have to constantly justify yourself.
>
> You have to accept that it goes with the territory and people have a right to question you. It does also mean that you can never switch off. Whenever I went on a family holiday, my children were under strict instructions not to tell anybody what I did. I knew the moment that anybody knew, I wouldn't get any peace.
>
> My most vivid memory of this was when I was head of children's TV and I had to sack Richard Bacon who had been taking cocaine and had been caught by the *News of the World*. We were going on holiday straight after and were on the flight to Tunisia where there was a complimentary copy of the *Daily Express* on every chair with Richard Bacon's face staring out from the front of every newspaper. I remember saying to my daughters, 'Just don't say a word.'

She found the experience demanded a careful balancing act. On the one hand, to take account of what everyone had to say was a guaranteed route to madness. On the other hand, to ignore their views totally would be an act of supreme arrogance that could place her dangerously out of touch. As she says:

> If you start to think people are going to think this of me, or that of me, therefore I am not going to make that decision, then you start to make the wrong decisions and will never get anywhere. In the end, the only judgement you have got is your own.

The answer, then, was to listen and to weigh up. What she wasn't doing was seeking immediate popularity by going with the loudest voices of the moment.

This seems to me the only way to operate. You stick to your guns when your gut instinct is telling you that you are right, but you engage with and listen to the views of the outside world too. In fact, if you get the balance right, external views actually help hone your instincts over time. Lorraine certainly found this – and never more so than when the idea for *Strictly Come Dancing* was first pitched:

> It is difficult to imagine a time when *Strictly Come Dancing* wasn't on the air, but it was an incredibly unusual idea. When it was first pitched to me, it was a very short pitch. The head of entertainment commissioning came to me and said that they had this great idea for a show called *Pro Celebrity Come Dancing*. I just loved the idea of celebrities learning to dance and could see that it could be quite glitzy and glamorous. I always have a sort of gut feeling when something is going to do quite well, although you never actually know when something is going to be a huge hit.

At that time we wanted to broaden out the entertainment on BBC One. We didn't have a big flagship entertainment show at that stage. I thought it would strike a bit of a chord and it was very different. The decision to commission the programme was literally made in a couple of seconds. It just felt right.

Once we commissioned it, the programme-makers who were working on it said, 'We have to have "celebrity" in the title.' I said, 'I am not having "celebrity" in the title,' and everybody kept saying to me, '*Pro Celebrity Come Dancing* is what it is.' I said, 'I don't care. As soon as "celebrity" is in the title, all the press will seize on it. It will be skewed negatively from the start and I am just not having it.' They thought I was being a real pain, and I was in a way, but I really dug my heels in. They kept coming up with other titles and nothing was right. Then somebody came up with *Strictly Come Dancing* and I said straight away, 'That is it.' That was the title. In a funny way, I think if it had been called *Pro Celebrity Come Dancing*, it might have failed.

Listening to the outside world but not being blown off course by its more extreme or vocal opinions is something at which Sir Terry Leahy was very adept during his time at Tesco. The supermarket giant is one of those companies whose very success has, in a peculiarly British way, brought criticism. It's praised for its extraordinary record of sustained growth and long-term profitability. But it also has its detractors who are concerned by two things: Tesco's extraordinary record of sustained growth and its long-term profitability.

DECISION-MAKING LESSONS

> Sometimes you do just have to be bloody-minded and bulldoze your way through, particularly when you are in a big organisation.

> The worst thing is to be surrounded by people who say yes, yes, yes and then go away and do absolutely nothing about it. It helps if you have a bit of an elephantine memory, so you can forget about things for a while and then go back and ask, What has happened to so and so?

Lorraine Heggessey, former chief executive,

Talkback Thames

Sir Terry himself was always careful not to be knocked off course by the naysayers:

You have to keep it in perspective. The view is overwhelmingly positive if you include ordinary people. Ninety five per cent of people like Tesco, while 5 per cent don't. It is just you can sometimes hear the 5 per cent more because controversy is more newsworthy.

In business, the rules of the competitive game are that you try to win customers and make a profit out of providing a service. Success is being good at that. So, it does throw you when you are criticised for being too good at something.

Some detractors are not persuadable and you have to accept that. The important thing is to make sure that the external pressures don't adversely affect internal confidence. People working in the stores don't like hearing about the company they work hard in every day being talked about in this way. I always tried to shield them from that.

Sir Terry has a sensibly unemotional approach to criticism:

I do try not to read too much press too. Or rather I don't read the press about myself, or pay too much attention to it. My belief is that journalists write articles and then forget about them. They don't intend for it to have the personal damage that it can have if people take it too seriously. Therefore, the best safeguard to that is: don't read it. I always get told about it anyhow, so I probably get it at about the force it was intended by getting it slightly second-hand. There is little point crucifying yourself by poring over every word.

Don't get blown off course

Everybody has an agenda, so it's essential when you're weighing up the validity of some critical remark or other that you understand why the person who made it did so.

Customer views really count. They're the people who are keeping you in business and they're the people who understand what you're about. They're the people who go on price comparison websites to check whether your unbeatable deal really is unbeatable. They're better informed now than they have ever been. I've already said that we monitor what customers say online because generally it's these forums that provide the first rumblings I'll hear of a problem that needs to be addressed.

Social media mechanisms are adept at extracting secrets that businesses would prefer to bury. They're the ones to highlight if, say, a company's delivery network is not up to scratch, or if customer service has always been a bit lethargic, or if a company is a little conservative with the truth when describing a product.

Consider the case of the Power Balance wristband, marketed by Power Balance Australia, which claimed that its holographic technology worked with the body's natural energy field to improve athletic performance. The wristband was heavily promoted through celebrity endorsements and viral marketing. However, the online community was having none of it. 'Where is the proof?' various bloggers demanded. Before long, the furore over the wristband caught the attention of mainstream media and everyone began questioning the claims. By December 2010, the Australian Competition and Consumer Commission forced the company behind Power Balance to publish a statement admitting that they had 'engaged in misleading conduct'. As Power Balance Australia found, you can't hide from criticism.

If you want to find out what's really going on, don't look at a company's carefully designed corporate website; trawl the Internet for tell-all pages of consumer complaints.

By contrast, the views of the media, of the City and of regulators need careful handling. The media are looking for a quick story, preferably a bad news story, and will then move on to something else. The city is generally looking for on-track earnings, and is impatient with those who don't deliver them. Regulators and external bodies often have an agenda that has almost nothing to do with the profitability or success of the organisation they're monitoring. None can be ignored, but if you allow them to dictate or change company policy you're asking for trouble.

Take the City, for example. Common sense dictates that you don't build shareholder value over weeks, or months. It takes years to build it in a way that is sustainable, and even great companies will have a blip or two over a five to seven year period. But that's not something that the City wants to hear, and it's something that business leaders battle with the whole time. Helen Weir, the former head of Lloyds retail banking empire and who also spent part of her career as finance director of Kingfisher, has long been an outspoken opponent of City short-termism:

> In my former roles as a finance director I had reservations about the move towards quarterly reporting, not because I didn't want performance information to be available, but because companies start managing to quarterly targets and that is not a good way to run a business. There is a risk that you just focus on a few short-term figures rather than doing the right things for business in the longer term.
>
> In my view, the role of short-termism in the City prior to and during the financial crisis has been underplayed. For instance, in the mid-2000s, in their desire to keep the City happy a number of banks made large mortgage market share commitments in mortgages. As a result, for a period of time in 2006 and 2007, mortgages were being written at negative margins, which just isn't sustainable. Many of these banks were the ones that subsequently ran into funding problems.
>
> Unfortunately, the pressure towards short-term reporting and ever increasing targets seems to have increased rather than abated.

So how do you deal with this? My view is that Sir Stuart Rose's robust approach is the one to go for:

> Investors should take the view that they are on the bus and in for the journey. If they believe that the journey is going to be one that is going to take them to a better place, with better scenery and a better end-point, then they should stick with it. Of course, everybody has got the right to get off at any point in the journey and say they don't want to go any further. But, they can't expect the bus to go a completely different route because they don't like the scenery. They shouldn't have got on the bus in the first place. They should get a different bus.

Sir Stuart, then, is adamant about who should be in the driving seat:

> I always say to shareholders who come to moan to me, 'If you don't like it, sell the shares and buy some other shares.' You cannot run your business at someone else's behest. You have to run it according to what you think is right.

Ignore the City and you win powerful enemies and outspoken critics. Allow the City to dictate what you do, however, and you become fixated on the next quarter's results, not on what brings about long-term success. That's not a strategy, and when it fails the City won't love you for that either.

Martha Lane Fox, the founder of lastminute.com, experienced this at first hand when, with her business partner Brent Hoberman, she faced an eleventh hour entreaty to raise the company's flotation price in March 2000. The pair had just completed an exhaustive road show promoting the share sale with institutional investors in the UK and America, and it had become apparent that there was huge demand. At 3 am, just hours before the shares were to be offered for sale, their advisers at Morgan Stanley were urging them to think again. The original range had been 190 pence to 230 pence, and now they were talking about 320 pence to 380 pence:

> The bankers were pushing and pushing to raise the price, which of course they would because that was their business. For us, though, it was a very hard decision and the stakes were high. We knew that an increased price would give the company the most money, but at the same time going for a lower price would give us a little bit of flexibility. There would be lower expectations and less pressure.

The float eventually went ahead at 380 pence and the share price jumped to 511 pence in the first hour's trading. Martha and Brent's decision was vindicated. When the dotcom bubble burst some time later, the shares dropped back considerably, perhaps further confirming the wisdom of having not over-egged the pudding when the company was floated:

> Our job was to put the company in the most robust position possible. At that moment in time the market was extremely buoyant and demand was high. It is easy to look back and say that it all collapsed later on. That is not the issue here. At that point we had just been on an extremely successful road show: everybody was upbeat about the business, lastminute.com was growing and we had to bank as much money as possible to keep

it in a secure financial position. Bearing all those factors in mind was why we made that decision.

In other words, as with everything to do with tough calls, there comes a point when you have to go with what every instinct in you tells you is the right thing. That may seem obvious, but that doesn't make it any less true. If you do go with what you feel is right, you'll get things wrong on occasion but you'll also be vindicated time and again.

I opened this chapter with Andy Clarke's unfortunate experience with the media over decisions he had made at Asda. I want to close it with the aftermath.

When the publicity firestorm hit, Andy had not only decided to improve what Asda had to offer, but was well on his way to executing the decision. As he recalls:

> What I knew then, but wasn't yet able to say, was we were just weeks away from launching our new high-quality, own brand, food range, Chosen by You, and I was really excited about it. I would have loved to have said that we have a programme to relaunch all our private label products, which we did, but we were not at a stage to be able to say it.

But because he had a good plan in place, he was able to turn things around within a matter of weeks:

> At the PR launch of Chosen by You three weeks later, it gave me the opportunity to say with a bit of a look and a smile, 'I know you read a few weeks ago what I said about food quality; well, it is a real shame that I couldn't have shown you this at the same

time because we are really excited about it.'

It was a good decision that paid off, with Asda showing steady sales growth in food in a particularly tough market thanks in great part to the 3,500-strong Chosen by You range. As Andy says, 'The bottom line is, we knew we had to fix these things and we already had.' Like all good decision-makers, however, Andy also learned a lesson from his experience:

> I don't want to be any less transparent and honest about the things I think we need to deliver and fix. I just now have to be careful about where and how I say it.

No decision-maker gets every aspect of every decision right every time. Good decision-makers, though, learn the whole time. Great decision-makers build on what they have learned.

Conclusion

What turns an everyday decision into a tough call?

It's not really a question of scale. A tough call can encompass anything from a decision to buy or sell a company to a decision to take action against an underperforming member of staff.

Nor is it a question of immediate circumstance. Many tough calls have to be made in difficult times, but they can crop up just as easily when things are otherwise going well.

No. In my view what characterises a tough call is that it's a decision that other people don't want to make. It may be that it's because they're intimidated by the scale of it. Or that they feel that they don't have enough information to go on. Or that they're terrified to get it wrong. Or that they think there could be several ways forward and they don't know which one to pick. Whatever the reason, it's left to a handful of people, and particularly the person at the top, to decide what to do.

There are many different ways to categorise these thorny decisions. In the first part of this book I've opted to identify four basic types – radical, crisis, opportunity and progress – but others see things slightly differently. BBC director general Mark Thompson, for example, distinguishes between two types of tough calls.

> **In the first instance, there are tough decisions which are difficult because the options are finely balanced and the arguments for doing this or that are very close. Oddly, a lot of these tough decisions are actually nice decisions to make. Suppose you were offered two jobs, for example. They may both be good positions and you may even secretly think it doesn't matter which one you take. But you still have to take a decision.**
>
> **The other sort of tough decisions can be easy in the sense that it is pretty clear what you should do, it is just that the consequences are so far-reaching and painful in human terms that it makes it really difficult. Even though actually you are pretty clear on what you need to do, it still feels pretty tough.**

However you divide things up, each category involves its own set of issues and difficulties. But in my view each demands the same basic sequence of actions on the part of the decision-maker:

1. Step in.
2. Collect and digest the best information available at the time.
3. Make the decision.
4. Communicate the decision.
5. Make sure it happens.
6. Move on.

Of all these stages, it tends to be stage 3 that people find hardest and that involves the greatest number of moving parts. But good decision-makers will bring a certain set of qualities to the table.

› They are never complacent when things are going well; they are always looking for the next opportunity or the next problem. Reality rules over optimism.
› They are never panicked when things are going badly; they continue to make decisions in a calm manner, but with the speed and urgency required.
› They do not shy away from making difficult calls or having difficult conversations.
› They are not intimidated by the prospect of asking others for their views, nor do they feel threatened by the fact that some may know more about a particular subject. They surround themselves with the best people they can find, listen to them, chew things over, then decide.
› They give their team the encouragement and room to hone their own decision-making skills.
› They are prepared to modify decisions as they are implemented but have the mental toughness not simply to go for consensus.
› They note, but refuse to be distracted by,

all the noise from outside the organisation that urges them to go one way or another.

› They always present a calm and confident front, even when they are not 100 per cent sure about whether something will work.

› They accept that mistakes will be made, but not that the same mistake will be made twice.

› They delegate tasks and decisions, but they never, ever delegate the responsibility for making a decision or executing it. They know that the buck always stops with the man or woman at the top.

› They know that they will rarely get any decision 100 per cent correct and that they will get some wrong.

› They know that they will always have to make a decision. Hedging your bets never works.

No two decision-makers display precisely the same characteristics. I tend to make my calls very quickly – something I learned at Mars, where the competitive atmosphere meant you needed to be quick on your toes, and where, because the company was privately owned, you weren't second-guessed by the outside world. Others like a more deliberate approach. All, though, know when and how to stick to their guns. And all appreciate how essential clear, decisive action is. As General Lord Richard Dannatt says:

> Pretty much anyone can muddle along when everything is going swimmingly and according to plan. The time that leaders really earn their pay is when the going gets tough. This is when the real qualities of a leader will out, when the real value is added and true leadership gets displayed.

Who's who

Marcus Agius (Barclays Bank)

Marcus Agius trained as a mechanical engineer at Cambridge, but spent 30 years of his working life at top drawer independent bank Lazards, rising to become chairman, before leaving to become chairman of Barclays in January 2007. Marcus, who has been dubbed the 'quintessential English banker', is also a senior non-executive director on the BBC's new executive board.

Surinder Arora (Arora Hotels)

Surinder Arora started his career as an office junior at British Airways while moonlighting as a hotel waiter. He invested all of his family's savings into property, eventually developing a row of houses opposite Heathrow Airport into a large-scale bed-and-breakfast operation. Following the demolition of the houses, it was on this site that his first hotel emerged in 1999 specifically for aircrews. In 2004, Arora International won the contract for a 605-bedroom, five-star hotel at Heathrow's new Terminal 5 development. The company currently has six directly managed hotels including sites at Gatwick, Heathrow and Manchester and around nine hotel developments in progress.

Ian Cheshire (Kingfisher)

After graduating from Cambridge with a degree in Economics and Law, Ian Cheshire learned about retailing with Guinness, which then ran a chain of convenience stores and newsagents. He then joined Sears as group commercial director, where he oversaw the demerger of Selfridges, before joining Kingfisher as group strategy director in 1998. He established his credentials as chief executive of Kingfisher's international operations, before eventually taking the top job at the DIY conglomerate in January 2008.

Andy Clarke (Asda)

After leaving King's School in Grantham, Lincolnshire, Andy began his career in retailing stacking shelves in Fine Fare at the age of 17. He joined Asda in 1992, as a store manager in Edinburgh, before taking on director roles in frozen food, bakery and produce. He left the supermarket group in 2001 to work at discount fashion chain Matalan and frozen food giant Iceland, before returning to Asda in 2005 as retail director. He was promoted to chief executive in May 2010.

Julia Cleverdon (Business in the Community)

Julia read History at Cambridge and got her first job in industry as a junior industrial relations officer at British Leyland. She says that it was here that she honed her skills persuading difficult individuals to get things done. From there she moved to the Industrial Society rising to become director of education. Julia was appointed chief executive of Business in the Community in 1992, where she significantly expanded the charity's work, earning a place on *The Times*' list of '50 most influential women in Britain'. She became Vice President of BITC in 2008 and a special adviser to Prince Charles on responsible business practice.

Adam Crozier (ITV)

After graduating from Edinburgh's Heriot Watt University, Adam Crozier moved into sales at Mars. He joined Saatchi & Saatchi as a media executive in 1988 and made it to the top – rapidly – becoming chief executive at the age of 31, after the founders left. He moved to the Football Association in 2000 and became chief executive of the Royal Mail in February 2003. He was involved in complex and sometimes controversial reform programmes at both organisations. In January 2010 it was announced that Adam was to become chief executive of ITV.

General Lord Richard Dannatt

Richard Dannatt was commissioned into The Green Howards regiment in 1971, after graduating from Durham University with a degree in Economic History. In his early years he served in Northern Ireland, where he was awarded the Military Cross at the age of 22, as well as in Cyprus and Germany. From 1994 to 1996 he was the commander of the 4th Armoured Brigade in Germany and Bosnia and in 1999 took command of the 3rd (United Kingdom) Division, also serving in Kosovo as Commander British Forces. Before taking command of NATO's Allied Rapid Reaction Corps he was the assistant chief of the general staff in the Ministry of Defence from 2001 to 2002. In March 2005 he became Commander in Chief, Land Command, before assuming the appointment of Chief of the General Staff in August 2006. In November 2011, Richard was named as a crossbench peer in the House of Lords.

Richard Desmond (Northern & Shell)

Richard Desmond left school at 14 and ran the cloakroom at a legendary rock venue in Manor House, north London, frequented by rock legends such as Hendrix, Zeppelin and The Who. Always keen on music, he had opened a record shop by the age of 21 and with his fledgling publishing group Northern & Shell, launched his first magazine International Musician in 1974. He then moved on to produce a range of weekly and monthly titles ranging from music to health, and finance to food and cooking. In 1993, Northern & Shell launched celebrity magazine OK! which began as a monthly magazine and grew to be the largest weekly magazine in the world. Richard bought Express Newspapers from United News and Media for £125 million in the year 2000 and ten years later, Northern & Shell acquired the Channel Five terrestrial television channel returning it to profit in a matter of months.

Charles Dunstone (Carphone Warehouse)

After leaving Uppingham School, where he had set up his first entrepreneurial venture selling pens and cigarette lighters, Charles Dunstone took a job with Japanese electronics giant NEC rather than go to university. In 1989, using £6,000 of savings, he opened his first Carphone Warehouse shop in Marylebone, London with the idea of opening up the fledgling mobile phone market to individual tradespeople. In 2008, Best Buy acquired 50 per cent of CPW's European and retail interests. Charles is also chairman of Talk Talk, the Prince's Trust and non-executive director of the *Daily Mail* and General Trust.

Val Gooding (former chief executive, BUPA)

Val Gooding began her career as a reservations agent for British Airways, working her way up through a number of senior positions, including head of cabin services and director of business units. After 23 years at BA, she quit to join BUPA in 1996 because she felt that spending her whole career with one company in one industry was too 'narrow'. After two years as managing director, UK operations, Val Gooding became chief executive, a position she held until retiring in 2008. Val, who was awarded the CBE for services to business in 2002, is now chairman of Premier Farnell PLC and a non-executive director of the BBC executive board, CBI, Standard Chartered Bank and the Lawn Tennis Association. She is also a trustee of the British Museum.

Moya Greene (Royal Mail)

Moya was born in Newfoundland and is a graduate of the Osgood Hall Law School. She began her career in the public sector, as an immigration adjudicator in Ottawa, moving on through positions in the

Department of Labour, Privy Council Office and then overseeing the privatisation of the Canadian National Railway. In 2003, the year she was named as among the 100 most influential women in Canada by the *National Post*, she joined engineering firm Bombardier as senior vice president. Two years later she became president and chief executive officer of *Canada Post*, where an aggressive cost-cutting campaign steered the organisation to a trebling of its net profits. In May 2010, she was named as chief executive of the Royal Mail.

Lorraine Heggessey (former chief executive, Talkback Thames)

After initially being rejected for a BBC news traineeship, following her graduation from Durham University with a degree in English Language and Literature, Lorraine began her career as a trainee journalist on the *Acton Gazette*. On her second application to the BBC, she was successful and spent 15 years in current affairs programming, rising to become a producer on the current affairs flagship *Panorama*. She then spent some time working outside of the BBC, on programmes such as *Hard News* and *Dispatches*, before returning to the BBC. She became head of Children's BBC in 1997 and was promoted to Director of Programmes and Deputy Chief Executive of the BBC's in-house production division two years later. She was promoted to controller of BBC One in November 2000, where one of her most notable successes was the re-commissioning of *Doctor Who*. In 2005, Lorraine left the BBC to become chief executive of Talkback Thames – producers of some of the UK's most popular programmes including *The X Factor* and *The Apprentice* – a position she held until June 2010, and is now a media consultant and public speaker.

Stephen Hester (RBS)

Stephen started his career at Credit Suisse First Boston, after graduating from Oxford with a first class honours degree in Politics, Philosophy and Economics. He rose steadily through the ranks, becoming chief financial officer and then global head of fixed income. He left in 2001 to become financial director of the then struggling Abbey National where he was instrumental in turning the bank around by restructuring its toxic debt. In 2004, after Abbey National was sold to Spain's Santander for £9.5 billion, Stephen was appointed chief executive of British Land. In November 2008, Stephen was appointed group chief executive of RBS.

General Sir Mike Jackson

General Sir Mike Jackson was born into a military family and began his army career at the age of 19 learning Russian in the Intelligence Corps at the height of the Cold War. The culmination of four decades in the army, including time as Commander Kosovo Force, Commander in Chief Land Command and Director General Development and Doctrine at the MoD, was to serve as Chief of the General Staff from 2003 to 2006. Believed to be one of the best-known British Generals since the Second World War, as head of the British Army Sir Mike dealt with claims of Iraqi prisoner abuse at the hands of UK troops and growing discontent about the role of coalition troops in the Middle East.

Justin King (Sainsbury's)

On graduating from Bath University Justin King joined Mars as a trainee, working first in production and then sales. After a brief spell with Pepsi and Häagen-Dazs, Justin King joined Asda, then at the beginning of its recovery process. In 2000, he joined Marks & Spencer as executive director in the food division. Four years on he was persuaded to join J. Sainsbury as chief executive to halt the slide in the grocer's market share. Since he joined he has made significant changes to the supermarket, including an aggressive price-cutting campaign whilst building on its quality ethical credentials, supply chain changes and the hiring of respected industry figures to the board.

Martha Lane Fox (founder, lastminute.com)

After graduating from Magdalen College, Oxford, Martha Lane Fox joined Spectrum management consultants, where she met her future business partner Brent Hoberman. Together in 1999 they set up lastminute.com, growing it into one of the UK's best-known internet businesses that floated at the height of the dotcom bubble and is still Europe's largest travel and leisure website. Martha stayed on as MD until 2003. In 2004, Martha was severely injured as a result of a car accident in Morocco – this resulted in over a year of hospitalisation and ongoing effects today. Since her recovery Martha has embarked on a number of entrepreneurial ventures, including founding the luckyvoice.com – a karaoke bar chain and online enterprise. She has also become non-executive director of Marks & Spencer and Channel 4. In June 2009, Martha was appointed the UK government's digital champion and has gone on to lead the high profile Race Online 2012 campaign – aiming to bring the benefits of the web to the nine million UK adults that have never been online.

Sir Terry Leahy (former CEO, Tesco)

Sir Terry Leahy read Management Science at the University of Manchester Institute of Science and Technology. He started his career as a product manager at the Co-op and joined Tesco as marketing executive in 1979. He became marketing manager in 1981, marketing director in 1992, deputy managing director in 1995 and chief executive at the age of 41. Under his leadership, Tesco has developed a market share as big as his two rivals put together and Sir Terry Leahy has been regularly voted as one of Britain's most admired business leaders. He stepped down as chief executive in March 2011.

Ian Livingstone (BT)

Graduating with a degree in economics, Ian Livingstone trained as an accountant with Arthur Andersen. After moving on to spend time at Bank of America and private equity firm 3i, Ian joined the Dixons group in 1991, rising to become the youngest FTSE 100 finance director at the age of 32. During his times as finance director, Dixons Group developed PC World and Freeserve and became market leader across a number of European customers. In 2002, he moved to BT as finance director, becoming chief executive of BT Retail in 2005 and succeeding Ben Verwaayen as group chief executive in 2008.

Carolyn McCall (easyJet)

Carolyn McCall began her career as a history teacher at Holland Park School in London. She joined the *Guardian* in 1986 and rose quickly through the ranks, becoming chief executive of Guardian Newspapers in 2000 and at the same time joining the board of the Guardian Media Group, the parent company. She became chief executive of Guardian Media Group in May 2006. In July 2010, Carolyn was appointed chief executive of budget airline group easyJet.

Martin McCourt (Dyson)

Martin's early career included roles as a general manager at Toshiba, national sales manager at Duracell, and sales and business development with Mars. Before joining Dyson in 1996, Martin spent two years as international development director and UK general manager for German stationers Pelikan. He was appointed chief executive of Dyson in 2001 where he has seen a ten-fold increase in the size of the business and diversification into 60 countries. In 2010, he was named Leader of the Year in the Orange National Business Awards.

James Murdoch (News Corp)

James Murdoch is the fourth of Rupert Murdoch's six children. He studied in Rome and considered becoming an archaeologist before signing up for Harvard. At the age of 27, James Murdoch moved to Hong Kong to take control of News Corp's ailing Asian satellite service Star TV. It was losing £100 million a year but was turned around to make a modest profit thanks to new channels and distribution deals with China, Taiwan and India. It has become a major source of profit growth for News Corporation, which in 2011 is set to deliver its highest annual profit ever. In 2003, James became chief executive of BSkyB and moved up to become chairman and chief executive of Europe and Asia for News

Corporation in 2007. In March 2011, he was appointed deputy chief operating officer, and chairman and CEO, international, News Corporation.

Jacques Nasser (BHP Billiton)

Born in Lebanon, Jacques Nasser moved with his family to Melbourne, Australia, at the age of four. His first job was at Ford of Australia after graduating from the Royal Melbourne Institute of Technology. Moving rapidly through the ranks, he held positions in Asia, South America, Europe and the US, before being named as president and chief executive of Ford in 1999. He stepped down in 2001. Jacques is chairman of BHP Billiton, a senior adviser at One Equity Partners, the private investment arm of JP Morgan, and is also a board member at British Sky Broadcasting.

Lord Gulam Noon (Noon Products)

Lord Gulam Noon ran the family food business in India for 20 years before leaving for the UK in 1969 with little money in his pocket. His first company, a confectionery business called Bombay Halwa Limited, grew rapidly from a single shop in Southall, London. He moved into ready meals in the 1980s after trying a supermarket curry which he thought was 'unattractive, insipid and badly packaged, a million miles from authentic Indian food'. From starting out with a workforce of 11 people, Noon Products grew to employ more than 1,250, supplying most of the UK's leading supermarkets. It was bought out by Kerry Foods in 2005.

Archie Norman (ITV)

Archie Norman was a member of a three strong team that established and built Kingfisher plc in the 1980s to become Britain's leading general merchandise retailer. In 1991, he took over as chief executive of ASDA and together with Allan Leighton lead the turnaround which, over eight years, transformed the business into the second largest supermarket group before being sold to Wal-Mart for an eight times multiple of the starting share price. Archie has also led the turnaround of Britain's third largest telecoms business Energis and Australian supermarket group Coles. He also served for eight years as a member of parliament, including as chief executive of the Conservative party and as a leading member of the shadow cabinet. Archie took over as chairman of ITV in January 2010 to recruit a new leadership team under Adam Crozier to lead a five-year transformation programme.

Dalton Philips (Morrisons)

Dalton, who is a graduate of University College Dublin and holds an MBA from Harvard, began his career as a store manager in 1992 in New Zealand with Jardine Matheson (the Hong Kong trading company). In 1998, he joined Wal-Mart in Brazil, eventually rising to the position of chief operating officer in Germany. Dalton was recruited by the Weston family in 2005 as chief executive of its Brown Thomas department store business in Ireland and in 2007 he moved to Canada to become chief operating officer of Loblaw, the Weston's supermarket business. In January 2010, it was announced that Dalton had been appointed as chief executive of Morrisons. With 20 years of retailing experience, Dalton has worked and lived in ten countries.

Feargal Quinn (Superquinn)

Feargal Quinn opened his first store in Dundalk at the age of 23, with the idea of specialising in fresh food. With the main focus on customer service, he pioneered in-store bakeries, pizza, pasta and even sausage kitchens, and eventually captured nine per cent of Ireland's grocery market. Feargal Quinn has also pursued a successful political career, as an independent member of the Senate, the upper house of the Irish parliament, since 1993.

Dame Gail Rebuck (Random House)

Gail Rebuck read Intellectual History at Sussex University. After a brief stint as a European tour guide and a retailer, she began her publishing career as a production assistant before Century Publishing founder Anthony Cheetham asked her to join him. Starting with a phone and a desk in a small room, they built a business which took over the far bigger Hutchinson, and which was subsequently bought by Random House in a £64.5 million deal in 1989. Gail Rebuck became chairman and chief executive of the Random House Group in 1991. Gail is a passionate believer in literacy and conceived World Book Day in 1998 and launched the Quick Reads charity in 2006.

Sir Stuart Rose (former chairman and chief executive, Marks & Spencer)

Stuart Rose first joined Marks & Spencer in 1972 as a management trainee, spending 17 years at the high-street giant before joining the Burton Group as chief executive. In 1997 he moved on to become chief executive of Argos, where he was unsuccessful in defending the company from a takeover bid by Great Universal Stores, but won respect for securing an increased price. He subsequently joined Booker, where he restructured the business and subsequently merged it with Iceland. He then moved on to be chief executive of Arcadia, restructuring and turning around the business before selling it to Philip Green in 2002. Stuart stepped down from his dual roles as chairman and chief executive of M&S in January 2011.

Sir Martin Sorrell (WPP)

Martin Sorrell read Economics at Christ's College Cambridge and has an MBA from Harvard University. He began his career at Glendinning, a marketing consultancy in Westport, Connecticut, before joining the sports agent Mark McCormack. He then worked for the retail entrepreneur Jimmy Gulliver before becoming finance director for the Saatchi brothers. While at Saatchis, Sorrell bought a company in Kent called Wire & Plastic Products, which made wire baskets for supermarkets. He joined WPP as chief executive in 1986 and transformed it by buying a string of marketing services companies. In 1987, he stunned the agency world with the hostile takeover of top ad agency J. Walter Thompson.

Two years later he succeeded in another dramatic takeover of Ogilvy and Mather, securing WPP's place as the major player in the global advertising market.

Mark Thompson (BBC)

Mark Thompson joined the BBC as a production trainee after graduating from Merton College, Oxford. Among various key roles, he was appointed editor of the *Nine O'Clock News* in 1988, editor of *Panorama* in 1990 and controller of BBC Two in 1996. By 2000 he was BBC director of television, but left the corporation in 2002 to become chief executive of Channel Four. He returned to the BBC as director general in May 2004 following a unanimous decision by the BBC Board of Governors which declared he had 'unquestionable public service credentials'.

Helen Weir (former group executive director (retail), Lloyds Banking Group)

Helen began her career as a management trainee at Unilever and then did an MBA at Stanford before working at management consultants McKinsey for five years. She moved from McKinsey to head B&Q's finance side and was promoted to finance director of its parent company Kingfisher in 2000. Helen was appointed as finance director of Lloyds TSB in 2004, and group executive director in charge of the retail bank in 2008 where she oversaw the integration of HBOS. Helen announced she was leaving Lloyds Banking Group in March 2011.

Index

Teena Lyons spent the early part of her career as a financial and consumer affairs journalist, writing for a number of national newspapers including the *Guardian,* the *Sunday Times* and *Daily Telegraph.* She also spent seven years as retail correspondent at the *Mail on Sunday,* where she broke a number of high-profile news stories as well as regularly interviewing the most important business leaders in the sector. Teena left Fleet Street in 2006 to write business books full-time and has since collaborated on a number of best-selling titles.